T0164026

CYCLING FOR COMPETITION

CYCLING FOR COMPETITION

ALL YOU NEED TO KNOW ABOUT EVERY TYPE OF RACING, FROM TRACK, ROAD RACING AND OFF-ROAD RACING TO CYCLO-CROSS AND TRIATHLON

TECHNIQUES, WINNING STRATEGIES, INDIVIDUAL TRAINING PLANS AND AN EXPERT GUIDE TO INTERNATIONAL RACES, ALL SHOWN IN 200 PHOTOGRAPHS

EDWARD PICKERING

southwater

This edition is published by Southwater, an imprint of Anness Publishing Ltd, Blaby Road, Wigston, Leicestershire LE18 4SE

Email: info@anness.com

Web: www.southwaterbooks.com; www.annesspublishing.com

If you like the images in this book and would like to investigate using them for publishing, promotions or advertising, please visit our website www.practicalpictures.com for more information.

Publisher: Joanna Lorenz
Project Editor: Anne Hildyard
Design: Steve West
Jacket Design: Nigel Partridge
Production Controller: Christine Ni

© Anness Publishing Ltd 2011

All rights reserved. No part of this publication may be reproduced, stored in a retrieval system, or transmitted in any way or by any means, electronic, mechanical, photocopying, recording or otherwise, without the prior written permission of the copyright holder.

A CIP catalogue record for this book is available from the British Library.

ETHICAL TRADING POLICY

At Anness Publishing we believe that business should be conducted in an ethical and ecologically sustainable way, with respect for the environment and a proper regard to the replacement of the natural resources we employ.
As a publisher, we use a lot of wood pulp in high-quality paper for printing, and that wood commonly comes from spruce trees.
We are therefore currently growing more than 750,000 trees in three Scottish forest plantations.
Because of this ongoing ecological investment programme, you, as our customer, can have the pleasure and reassurance of knowing that a tree is being cultivated on your behalf to naturally replace the materials used to make the book you are holding.
For further information about this scheme, go to www.annesspublishing.com/trees

Previously published as part of a larger volume, *The Complete Practical Encyclopedia of Cycling*

PUBLISHER'S NOTE

Although the advice and information in this book are believed to be accurate and true at the time of going to press, neither the authors nor the publisher can accept any legal responsibility or liability for any errors or omissions that may be made nor for any inaccuracies nor for any loss, harm or injury that comes about from following instructions or advice in this book.

CONTENTS

Introduction

As soon as bicycles had evolved enough to go fast, people started racing them. Pierre Michaux's velocipede was invented in 1861, and within 10 years the first recorded race had taken place. The popularity of that event confirmed bicycle racing as a sport.

Bike racing is enjoying a real renaissance in Europe and the United States, owing to the success and popularity of Lance Armstrong, who won the Tour de France seven times, and UK success in the Olympics in 2008. To succeed at racing, you need to set even tougher targets, and have the discipline to train effectively and regularly. But you will be taking part in the most rewarding sport of all.

Whatever level you decide is suitable for you to attempt, there is a whole world out there for you to discover on two wheels.

Cycling for competition began in Saint-Cloud Park, in Paris, on 31 May 1869, when the first velocipede race took place – a 1,200m (0.75 mile) event, with James Moore, an expatriate English doctor, taking first place. Since 1,200m was well below the distance potentially covered by a bicycle in one day, it wasn't long before races were being run between separate towns. The inaugural Paris–Rouen race, also in 1869, covered

122km (76 miles). Moore won that race, too. Considering that pneumatic tyres were yet to be invented, then the average speed of 11kph (7mph) recorded by Moore becomes even more impressive.

Bicycle racing became more and more popular in the last decade of the 19th century, with massed-start races drawing huge crowds and competitors from all over Europe. Place-to-place events were the biggest draw, and distance was no object to the organizers of these events. Bordeaux–Paris, raced for the first time in 1891, covered a gruelling 600km (373 miles). Another Englishman, George Pilkington-Mills, raced through the night to win the race in just over 24 hours. Although another Briton, Arthur Linton, won five years later, only one more would win the race before the final running of the event in 1988 – Tom Simpson in 1963. The same year saw the even longer Paris–Brest–Paris event, which covered 1,200km

Above: Fausto Coppi, one of the first great champions of road racing. Coppi captured the heart of post-war Italy when he won the Tour of Italy in 1955.

(745 miles) across northern France, and was won in 71 hours by Frenchman Charles Terront. This event still exists as a four-yearly endurance test for amateur cyclists.

Professional races

The oldest professional race that is still running on an annual basis is the Liège–Bastogne–Liège Classic, which began in Belgium in 1892, and was won for three years in a row by the Belgian cyclist Leon Houa. Liège–Bastogne–Liège was run only five more times before 1919, but it then became an annual fixture and remains one of the most important bike races in the world.

The most renowned one-day classic is the Paris–Roubaix race, which first took place in 1896. To this day, it still uses the old cobbled forest roads of industrial northern France, and has the nickname

Left: The Tour de France in 1964, going along a scenic but challenging part of the route.

the 'Hell of the North'. Racing over cobbled roads is a different proposition from racing on smooth tarmac – Paris–Roubaix is a race that tests cyclists to their limits.

At the turn of the 20th century, bike races were still organized on a place-to-place basis, but a stroke of marketing genius in November 1902 changed the nature of bike racing forever.

Henri Desgrange, a journalist for French newspaper *L'Auto*, came up with the idea of a bike race around France for July 1903 – not just from one place to another, but around the entire country – as a means of promoting the newspaper. The distance – 2,414km (1,500 miles) – was massive, so Desgrange split the race into six stages, starting in Paris, then heading to Lyon, Marseille, Toulouse, Bordeaux and Nantes before returning to Paris. The stages might have been designed to break up the race, but the distances were still huge – the longest stage, between Nantes and Paris, was 471km (292 miles).

Above: Eddy Merckx, winning his first Tour de France in 1969. He set a record that remains unbroken.

Below: Crowds line a mountainous stretch of the road to see the competitors pass by in the 1949 Tour de France.

The world stage

In the early part of the 20th century, more and more stage races sprang up around Europe. The Giro d'Italia, or Tour of Italy, which is generally considered to be the second most important Grand Tour after the Tour de France, was started in 1909, while the Vuelta a España, Spain's version, followed suit in 1935. Meanwhile, important one-day races, such as the Tour of Lombardy and Milan–San Remo in Italy, and the Tour of Flanders in Belgium, became established.

As the races grew in size, the riders themselves became famous. Before and after World War II, the rivalry between two Italian riders, Gino Bartali and Fausto Coppi, divided the nation.

Bartali, a staunch Catholic with a modest and conservative disposition, attracted older fans, while the secular Coppi, who created a scandal by divorcing his wife – an unpopular move in religious Italy – was identified with by younger, more progressive Italians. The two went head to head in the 1949 Giro d'Italia, and Coppi thrashed his older rival.

Coppi's 1952 Tour de France win is renowned as being one of the best of all time. The organizers had introduced tough stages through the Pyrenees and

Alps since the 1910 race. But in 1952 they made another important development – the summit finish. With stages to ski resorts such as

Above: Eddy Merckx, shown in 1974 in Vouvray, Orléans, is held to be the best-ever racing cyclist.

Alpe d'Huez, the final kilometres were all uphill, which made the race even harder. Coppi won at Alpe d'Huez, which has become a regular fixture on the Tour, and dominated the race.

The first rider to win the Tour five times was Frenchman Jacques Anquetil, between 1957 and 1964, while his compatriot Bernard Hinault in the 1970s and 1980s and Spaniard Miguel Indurain in the 1990s also won five Tours. The two most famous multiple winners of the Tour were Belgian cycling star Eddy Merckx and American Lance Armstrong (see boxes).

Now, the Tour is a multi-million-euro affair that captures the attention of sport fans every summer. From humble beginnings in 1869, competition cycling has become a global sport.

Right: Tom Boonen rides on cobbled roads in the Paris–Roubaix race in 2004.

Eddy Merckx

Belgian cyclist Eddy Merckx was the first international superstar of bicycle road racing. During a professional career spanning 13 years from 1965 to 1978, he won a record number of races – as many as 575, according to some – including five Tours de France.

Merckx's nickname was 'the Cannibal' – he had as insatiable an appetite for being the winner of bike races as Muhammad Ali had for winning boxing fights. His racing style was aggressive, and he would often attack a long way from the finish.

Early in his career, he took victories in prestigious one-day races like Milan–San Remo and Paris–Roubaix. He also won three world championships, a record equalled, but never beaten. To add to his five Tour de France wins, he also won five Tours of Italy (Giro d'Italia) and one Tour of Spain (Vuelta a

España) – no cyclist in history has come anywhere close to matching Merckx's 11 victories in Grand Tours.

But it was the Tour de France that defined Merckx's career. He won his first Tour in 1969, at his first attempt, and took his fifth and final win in 1974, equalling the record of five overall wins set by the Frenchman Jacques Anquetil.

Merckx's first Tour de France in 1969 was one of the most dominant victories in the history of the race. As well as winning the yellow jersey (awarded to the rider who covers the course in the best time), he won the green jersey (for the points classification) and the polka-dot jersey of the King of the Mountains. No other rider has achieved this feat. He also won a record 34 stages of the Tour de France in his career.

Lance Armstrong

Eddy Merckx may have won more races in the course of his career than Lance Armstrong, but it is the American who has achieved more worldwide fame.

Armstrong was a precocious Texan who started his sporting career as a triathlete, but focused on bike racing in his early 20s. He exploded on to the world of professional cycling when he won the world championships in 1993 at the age of 21, but although he had won individual stages in the Tour de France, he was not considered a likely winner of the coveted yellow jersey.

In 1996, Armstrong was diagnosed with cancer, and given only a slim chance of staying alive, let alone recovering enough to resume his racing career. But he battled the disease, undergoing extensive chemotherapy, and made a comeback as a professional in 1998. He surprised many people by riding to fourth place in the Tour of Spain that year, and appeared at the 1999 Tour de France as an outsider. Armstrong went on to dominate the race, gaining time in both the individual time trials and in the mountain stages, and gained worldwide coverage for his comeback from cancer. He won the next six Tours after that, taking his seventh and final yellow jersey in 2005, establishing a record that will probably never be equalled, let alone beaten. In winning seven Tours, he established a new tactic, using his team to control the opposition before landing the killer blow himself.

In retirement, Armstrong continues to be an influential spokesman in the fight against cancer. He probably summed it up best himself when he said, "cancer chose the wrong guy".

Right: Lance Armstrong, an indomitable sportsman, who won the Tour de France a record-breaking seven times in consecutive years.

GETTING READY TO RACE

For some people, racing is the purest expression of bicycle riding. The bicycle was invented to be an efficient machine, and nowhere is this more important than in a bike race, when man and machine strive to be the fastest and best. No sooner had the bike been invented than people began to wonder how fast they could go and who could ride the fastest. As technology improved, other branches of bike racing evolved. Racing demands specific skills, and the next section explains how to develop them.

Left: Bike racing on- or off-road takes dedication and determination.

Weight Training for Cyclists

Cycling is the best training for cycling. If you are planning on entering an enduro (off-road race) or a sportive, there is no substitute for miles on a bike. However, it is a good idea to complement your cycling with other forms of training if you have the time for it.

Weight training is a good method to give yourself all-round body strength, but cyclists should not do too much of this kind of exercise. The more bulk you build through weight training, the heavier you will become, which means more body weight to carry up hills. Don't overdo it.

For the best results in terms of strength, you should focus on three different sets of exercises when you are weight training to improve your performance as a cyclist. These are: leg exercises, which will enable you to ride more strongly; upper body exercises, because the arms have to work quite hard to support the body on the bike; and core exercises, to strengthen the abdominal muscles and the back and which will provide a strong 'anchor' for the legs to work against.

When weight training, always start out under the guidance of a qualified instructor and take his or her advice to devise a programme of training. Start off with three sets of 12 repetitions of each exercise, using a weight that is half of the maximum you can manage. Increase weights gradually, and move up to three sets of 15 repetitions.

Always warm up thoroughly. Either cycle to the gym or try cycling on a stationary bike for at least 15 minutes. After a weight training session, do a series of stretches, and warm down, either on a stationary bike, or by cycling home.

Leg strength exercises

Strengthens: Hamstrings

Hamstring curl
Put your feet between the pads. Pull up, bend the leg until the calf muscle almost touches the back of the thigh. Release.

Leg extension

Strengthens: Quadriceps

Prepare by hooking your feet under the machine, holding on to the handles and bracing against the back. With toes pointing slightly outward, extend your lower leg until your leg is straight, then let the weight down again.

Squat

Strengthens: Quadriceps

Face forward with feet 15cm (6in) apart. Squat until your thighs are parallel with the ground. Keep your back straight. Stand up slowly, keeping your back straight. Don't lock out the knees and don't let the knees bend outward.

Leg press

Strengthens: Quadriceps

Sit with your feet 15cm (6in) apart on the plate. Push up until your legs are straight. Let the weight down until your knees are bent at about 90 degrees. Push up again. Keep the knees working in a straight line parallel with your feet.

Heel raise

Strengthens: Calf muscles

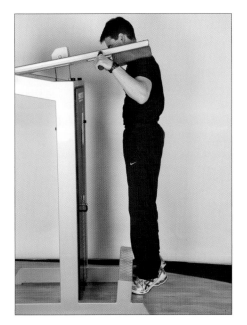

Stand with your toes on a step, with a weight across your shoulders, feet 15cm (6in) apart. Rise up until you are on tiptoes, then lower yourself down.

Crunch

Strengthens: Abdominal muscles

Lie flat on the ground with knees bent at 90 degrees. With your hands behind your head, slowly lift your shoulders off the floor. Lower the head back to the floor.

Back extension

Strengthens: Lower back

Lie on your front with the upper body hanging down. Brace feet against the supports. Slowly raise the upper body until almost straight. Lower back down.

Lat pulldown

Strengthens: Latissimus dorsi

Brace your legs under the support, reach up with straight arms and hold the bar with hands shoulder-width apart. Pull the bar down until it touches your chest. Let it back up slowly. Keep a straight back for the exercise.

Bench press

Strengthens: Pectorals, shoulders

Hold the weight and raise it with your hands above your shoulders, then push up until your arms are straightened, but don't lock them out completely. Carefully lower the weight until the bar just touches your chest.

Seated row

Strengthens: Shoulders, upper arms

Sit on a mat on the floor, with a straight back, feet braced against the footrests with knees slightly bent. Pull the bar toward the lower chest with the upper body still, until your hands touch your chest. Release slowly.

Stretches for Cyclists 1

Stretching helps loosen muscles and prevents the risk of sudden injury from working them too hard too quickly. To avoid injury and to gain the most from your workouts, you need to warm up and warm down properly.

Tight muscles can reduce power, co-ordination and endurance, all qualities that are necessary for cyclists.

To compensate for this, it is necessary to follow a regular routine of stretching, which will increase flexibility. Being more flexible will aid your recovery from workouts, and give you good posture and confidence to go with your increased energy levels and fitness.

With stretching, little and often is better than a long session once a week. By spending just 15 minutes after each training session stretching your muscles, you can make a big difference in your body's flexibility.

When performing the stretches on the next few pages, stretch until you feel the muscle tightening, relax your breathing, and hold the position for 15 seconds. Then release slowly. Don't bounce, or move too fast. Instead, gradually employ your muscles' full range of movement, and stay relaxed. Don't tense up any other muscles and don't hold your breath.

You should also be aware that stretching is not always a good idea. Never stretch when your muscles are 'cold', and listen to your body's reaction to stretching. If you feel sudden pain, stop the stretch and ensure that you have not injured yourself. Cyclists need to pay particular attention to the hamstrings and lower back. Tightness in one of these areas can lead to tightness or injury in the other. The hamstrings are not fully extended when cycling, and the repetitive nature of the cycling motion will eventually lead to your hamstrings becoming much less supple.

Stretch after your rides, but also after weight-training sessions, and any other exercises. For a little time and effort, you can gain flexibility, and prevent injury. Proper preparation is vital for anyone wanting to get fit. Going straight into a hard workout without warming up puts you at risk of injury and you will not be able to perform so well during your training session. If you finish your workout without warming down, your legs will be stiffer afterward and probably also the next day – if you have a workout planned for that day, it will not be as effective, because your muscles will be too tired to work properly.

A typical training session	
Minutes	**Activity**
15	Warm up on the bike
50	LSD ride including 30-minute tempo riding session
15	Warm down on the bike
10	Stretch
Total:	90 minutes

Warming up

To warm up, simply ride slowly, steadily increasing your workload until you can feel yourself breathing a bit more heavily. Once you get to this level, which should take about 5 minutes, maintain the same effort for another 10 minutes. Concentrate, focus and relax, especially if you have a difficult workout coming up. While your body warms itself up, your mind should be preparing itself for the workout. Warming up gets the metabolism fired up and ready to deal with the bigger effort that is going to follow. Your body temperature will rise, your heart will start to send more blood around your body and this will prepare your system for your training session.

Winding down

Once you have finished your workout, you need to put the same principle into reverse. Simply wind down by riding the last 15 minutes of your ride in a low gear, spinning your legs out at an easy speed. This allows your body to flush out some of the waste products that build up in your muscles during hard exercise. A short warm-down after every ride will reduce any leg stiffness you may have.

The advantage of cycling is that you can do your warming up and warming down on the bike – just build in about 15 minutes' worth of riding distance on to the front and back end of your ride, and the job is done.

Stretch after exercise

The best time to stretch is while your body is still warm after your workout. If this is impractical, stretch in the evening, after taking a warm shower or bath. Do as many of the stretches illustrated here as possible, paying particular attention to your legs and the lower back. If you feel you are especially inflexible or want to develop your stretching routine, speak to a physiotherapist, who will be able to advise you on specific exercises for parts of the body.

Above: Weight training and stretching will help to improve your performance on the bike by making you stronger and more flexible.

Head stretch

Stretches: Neck

Tilt head sideways to the left then the right then forward to stretch the back of the neck. Hold 5 seconds. Then tilt the head backward. Hold for 5 seconds.

Gluteal stretch

Stretches: Gluteus maximus

Stand on one leg, bend it slightly, then rest your other ankle on the thigh. Bend forward until you feel the stretch in the buttock of the leg you are standing on.

Lateral leg stretch

Stretches: Long adductors, inner thigh

Place the feet wide apart and lean forward so your body weight rests on your hands. Widen your stance. Rotate hips inward to stretch each leg in turn.

Quad pull-up

Stretches: Quadriceps

Stand on one leg, and bend the other leg up behind you. Grasp the foot and pull up until you can feel the quadriceps stretching. Stretch out the other arm for balance. To increase the stretch, pull the foot up higher. Repeat with the other leg.

Side lunge

Stretches: Inner thigh

Place feet wide apart, bend one knee so your weight goes down on it. Lower your bottom as far as you can toward the floor with your arms out straight and hands clasped for balance. Keep other leg straight. Repeat on other side.

Touching toes

Stretches: Hamstrings

With feet slightly apart and legs straight, raise arms above your head, stretch so the back lengthens, then bend down as far as you can toward your toes. Don't bend the knees. Hold for 15 seconds, breathing steadily, then stand upright.

Stretches for Cyclists 2

Specific stretches will help to improve your flexibility when you are cycling. Because the range of movement on a bike is limited – your legs don't fully extend through the pedal stroke – the muscles become stronger but tighter. These lunges and stretches aim to stretch all of the body.

Forward lunges

Stretches: Hip flexor

Put one leg in front, the other behind, and bend your front knee, keeping your back straight. Lower yourself until the knee of your back leg touches the floor.

Follow the exercise on the left: one leg in front with knee bent, and touching the floor with the other knee. For extra stretch, raise your hands as far as you can above your head.

Abdominal stretch

Stretches: Abdominal muscles

Lie on a mat on the floor, on your front with your knees, toes and chest touching the floor, and hands beside your chin.

Push up with your arms and bend the back, stretching the abdominal muscles. Keep your head level, facing forward.

Ankle rotation

Stretches: Calf muscles, shins

Place hands on the hips for balance. Lift left foot off the ground. Keep the other leg straight and still and rotate the left foot widely around the ankle. Change to the other side and repeat the exercise.

Calf stretch

Stretches: Calf muscles

Lean with your hands against a wall with one leg stretched out behind you and the other supporting you. Push down with the heel of your straight leg, and use your arms to get closer to the wall.

Lat stretch

Stretches: Latissimus dorsi

With hands shoulder width apart, hold a horizontal bar above your head. Let your weight suspend from the arms, to stretch the upper back and shoulders. Rest and repeat but don't overdo it.

Shoulder stretch

Stretches: Posterior shoulder

Bring one arm across your chest, just below the horizontal level. Hook the other arm around so your straight arm rests in the crook of the elbow. Use your bent arm to pull the other arm towards the body. Repeat on the other side.

Bicep stretch

Stretches: Biceps

Stretch your arm out as straight as you can behind you at shoulder height. Place your hand on a wall. Rotate your hand anticlockwise. You will feel a stretch in your biceps. Repeat the exercise using the other arm and hand.

Wrist stretch

Stretches: Forearms

Have arms straight in front of you, the palms facing outwards and the backs of the hands facing each other. Put the right hand over the left, so the palms meet, and clasp fingers. Pull hands under and towards you. Swap hands.

Cross-training for Cyclists

For racing cyclists, training on the bike and following a regime of weight training leave little time for other sports. However, taking part in other sports can help improve your overall fitness, flexibility and co-ordination.

For the keen leisure cyclist, sportive and enduro rider, playing other sports can help to improve cycling fitness and all-round fitness. Some sports can even be linked with cycling. Triathlons, which combine swimming, cycling and running, and duathlons, which involve both running and cycling, are currently enjoying a boom.

Both swimming and running are endurance sports, which means that training in these two sports will increase non-specific cardiovascular fitness, with possible benefits for cycling. These two activities also use muscle groups that cycling under-uses, which leads to greater all-round fitness and helps prevent injury.

Other sports are also good for cycling. Any team sport that involves running will boost fitness and all-round flexibility. Ball games are good for hand–eye co-ordination and balance, which will contribute to developing better bike-handling skills.

Above: Running regularly boosts endurance and offers an alternative to bike training when riding is impractical. Left: Racket sports like badminton and tennis help co-ordination and flexibility.

Swimming and running

If you have been cycling for a long time, the first thing you need to be aware of is that years of not doing any running-based sports will leave you susceptible to muscle strains, injuries and stiff legs. Before embarking on other sports, start increasing the amount of time you spend stretching.

The easiest sports for cyclists to relate to are swimming and running, which involve similar training regimes. Running uses a different set of muscles from cycling, so the important thing is to build up slowly. Buy a good pair of training shoes for running in, and for your first run, go out for a 20-minute session. Spend the first 5 minutes walking fast, then jog slowly for 10 minutes. Finally, walk for the last 5 minutes. Remember to stretch, emphasizing the legs.

The next day, go for an easy bike ride, at LSD tempo at the most. This will help your legs to recover. You may experience stiffness, especially if you ran too fast, so spin the stiffness out with some familiar cycling movement. Stretch.

Build up your running until you reach a point where you can go for a 45-minute run with no after-effects. Then you can include a couple of runs a week in your cycling training. The advantage of running is that it is much more labour-intensive than cycling – you can get the same amount of exercise in a 30-minute run as you can in 1 hour of cycling. If you are busy, running is a good way to maintain fitness for cycling.

Sports for cyclists				
Sport	**Endurance**	**Flexibility**	**Co-ordination**	**Agility**
Badminton	-	X	X	X
Cricket	-	-	X	-
Football	-	-	X	X
Martial arts	-	X	X	X
Mountaineering	X	-	-	-
Rock climbing	-	X	X	X
Rugby	-	-	X	-
Running	X	-	-	X
Swimming	X	X	-	-
Taiko drumming	-	X	X	-
Tennis	-	-	X	X
Triathlon	X	X	-	-
Ultimate Frisbee	-	X	X	X

Swimming is initially difficult for cyclists because it makes much more use of the upper body, whereas cycling emphasizes the legs. Swimming workouts also strengthen the core muscles, which will contribute to a stronger cycling style. Training for swimming also trains the mind to be more conscious of exercise economy. The more economical a cyclist is, and the more efficient his or her style, the faster they will go for the same effort. With swimming, brute strength and high fitness levels count for much less than technique and skill. By working on the correct technique, a swimmer uses his or her fitness to maximum advantage. By applying lessons like this to cycling, you can improve cycling efficiency.

Other sports
Ball sports such as football and racket sports like tennis are also good for cyclists, offering a full physical workout. Co-ordination and agility from catching or aiming at a fast-moving object results in better reflexes and balance, and helps with bike handling and manoeuvring.

Top: Rock climbing improves balance, co-ordination and overall body strength. Above: Swimming helps to increase upper body strength and endurance.

The most important aspect of cross-training may not be the physical benefits of extra co-ordination, flexibility and endurance, but mental benefits. The training for cycling can be very serious, especially for difficult workouts. Cross-training lets cyclists enjoy sport without the pressure of performing. This can have a positive effect on mental attitude.

Keeping a Training Diary

It is important for cyclists to have long-term goals. Riding week-in, week-out can be lots of fun, but building up towards a goal is a way of getting more satisfaction and a sense of achievement out of the sport.

If you decide what you want to achieve and build up to, it is a good idea to keep a training diary. This allows you to record your progress, and to plan your workouts around your goal.

If your goal is to finish a 170-km (105-mile) mountainous sportive in four months' time, and you can currently ride 100km (62 miles) before fatigue sets in, plan to increase your longest ride distance on a weekly basis until the final run-up to your event. Write your plan into your training diary, and then, as each day passes, you can write in the actual workout you did on each day. You will have a record of whether or not you are on track.

Below: Once you have a goal in mind, you can plan your training accordingly, never losing sight of the end point.

Above: All serious racing cyclists keep a training diary, to plan workouts, and to get to know their reaction to training schedules.

What to put in your training diary
Use the sample training diary opposite as a schedule for a week's training. Fill in the gaps each day. If you wish, add your own supplementary pages and end up with a record of your training activities.

At the front of the diary, insert a printout of the current year, with months across the top and days down the side. Next, write in your main goal or goals for the year. This will give you an idea of how long you have until you need to be at peak fitness, and also a good idea of how your training is going. As you cross off the days, you can compare how you are progressing with how long you have to go.

Next, print out sheets of paper similar to the diary pictured here. Each page covers one week, with space for scheduled workouts, actual workouts and all other information that you need. At the start of each week list your aims, either short- or long-term, for that week. They could include at least one long ride, two hill sessions, a fartlek session, or whatever you have planned. Your initial goal could be to ride in a build-up event for your main goal.

Take your pulse

Each day, on waking, check and write in your weight and resting pulse rate. These are good indications of your condition. A high pulse rate could indicate that you are fatigued or feeling stressed. Significant weight loss could mean that you have been training hard and need to back off for a couple of days. Once you have been up for an hour or so, give yourself a mark out of 10 for your energy level. Are you raring to go and bouncing around the house, or are you feeling flat and listless?

This score is a subjective mark, but seeing how you react physically to your training is important for gauging how hard you need to make it for further sessions. If you have two weeks of very hard training, and then take two days off, an easy day the next day and then feel 10 out of 10 on the fourth, that's a good indicator that your training has paid off. It also shows that after a hard series of workouts you feel recovered and strong by the fourth day – this information might help with peaking for your goal.

Plan ahead

For each day, write in your scheduled workout – this can be done well in advance, but it is best to leave it until you have at least started that week, so your planning can be as accurate as possible. Then, as each day passes, enter what you actually achieved. Perhaps you planned a 2-hour workout, but had to stay late at the office and only had time for an hour. Don't berate yourself for missing the training, just keep a record of what happened and see if you can compensate another day.

Lastly, at the end of the week fill in a summary of the total number of hours' training, the distance covered, your weight (including any gain or loss) and body fat percentage, if you have the means to measure it.

Over the long-term, by keeping a record of your training, you can chart your progress, and work out what training strategy will work best for you. The information gained also helps you to plan your training into the future.

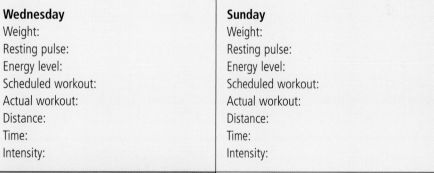

Sample training diary

Date:

Aims for the week:

1 One long ride
2 Four rides total
3 Stretch every day

Monday
Weight:
Resting pulse:
Energy level:
Scheduled workout:
Actual workout:
Distance:
Time:
Intensity:

Tuesday
Weight:
Resting pulse:
Energy level:
Scheduled workout:
Actual workout:
Distance:
Time:
Intensity:

Wednesday
Weight:
Resting pulse:
Energy level:
Scheduled workout:
Actual workout:
Distance:
Time:
Intensity:

Thursday
Weight:
Resting pulse:
Energy level:
Scheduled workout:
Actual workout:
Distance:
Time:
Intensity:

Friday
Weight:
Resting pulse:
Energy level:
Scheduled workout:
Actual workout:
Distance:
Time:
Intensity:

Saturday
Weight:
Resting pulse:
Energy level:
Scheduled workout:
Actual workout:
Distance:
Time:
Intensity:

Sunday
Weight:
Resting pulse:
Energy level:
Scheduled workout:
Actual workout:
Distance:
Time:
Intensity:

Summary
Hours trained:
Kilometres ridden:
Weight:
Body fat percentage:

Left: It is easier to assess your fitness day by day and month by month when you fill in a training diary.

ROAD RACING

The thrill of the road race has few equals in modern
sport. As part of a multi-coloured pack, riders fly up hills
before swooping down the other side, and cruise for
miles at great speeds before unleashing a fearsome dash
for the line. Finishing a road race takes more
than great speed and stamina. A number of riding skills
are needed to survive in a road race – how to climb,
how to descend, how to infiltrate a breakaway,
how to outsprint your rivals, and how to use team
tactics to your advantage.

Above: Road racers round a sharp bend in a mountainous race.
Left: Professional bike racers are among the fittest athletes on the planet.

The Road-racing Bicycle

Road-racing bikes are sleek, lightweight and fast. Ergonomic and aerodynamic principles are used in design so that everything possible is honed to a minimum, in order for the rider to be able to generate more speed.

Each element in a racing bike has been designed to be lightweight so that the rider can achieve maximum speed and responsive handling.

Frames

Carbon fibre or aluminium are used to make frames, or even a combination of the two, in which the main triangle of the frame is stiff aluminium, while the forks and seat stays are carbon fibre, to absorb some of the road shock. Frame tubes are wider than traditional steel bikes because aluminium is so much lighter than steel. Larger diameter tubes are stiffer, but even though more material is used in their construction, they are still much lighter than a comparative steel frame.

Right: A lightweight front mech (mechanism) on a racing bicycle.

Anatomy of a racing bike

❶ Wheels: size 700x20c, with 24 spokes and slick, lightweight tyres. Having a narrow section is much more aerodynamic.
❷ Frame: Carbon fibre or aluminium, with compact design and sloping top tube.
❸ Brakes: High performance dual pivot calliper. Carbon fibre brake levers to save weight.

❹ Chainrings: 53–42, attached to hollow bottom bracket axle and hollow cranks to save weight.
❺ Sprockets: 10-speed freewheel with 12–21 block.
❻ Gear changers: Brake levers also function as gear changers when they provide instant gear-changing ability.

❼ Saddle: Narrow and hard, with titanium seat rails to save weight.
❽ Handlebars: Dropped carbon fibre handlebars with ergonomically designed tubes for more comfortable and effective riding.
❾ Pedals: Lightweight pedals with special bindings for shoeplates to clip into.

The modern trend is for sloping top tubes and compact frames, which are smaller than traditional frames. A compact frame is stronger, because the tubes are shorter. They also allow frame manufacturers to make frames in fewer sizes, with most compact frames coming in three different sizes. Individual riders can tailor their position with precision using seatpins, stem, cranks and handlebars. Clearances between wheels and frame are reduced to almost nothing, and the profile of the bike is as narrow as possible, for better aerodynamics.

Specifications of wheels

Wheels are narrow – 700x20c, with 24 spokes, or fewer for the front wheel, depending on the model and spoke pattern. Tyres are slick and lightweight, with little or no tread – with such a small area of the tyre on the road at any one time, this actually offers the best grip. The fastest tyres used to be one-piece tubulars, which were extremely lightweight and glued to the wheel. However, the performance of traditional tyres, with a wire-on outer layer and inner tube, is now similar to tubular tyres. Wire-on tyres are easier to mend.

Components

Gearing in a racing bike is higher than the bikes that have been covered so far – road-racing bikes need to travel at high speeds, and the pace is rarely slow enough in a road race to justify using very low gears. Even on climbs, the riders try to go up so fast that their bottom gear doesn't need to be super-low. A typical racing bike has 52 or 53–42-tooth chainrings on the front, although this can be adapted to 53–44 if the course is less hilly, or 53–39 if it is especially hilly. At the back, a typical block would be 12–21 or 12–23, depending upon the type of terrain. Professional sprinters use an 11-tooth sprocket, but you should be very fit and strong before you attempt to turn over such a large gear. Brakes are lightweight and high performance.

Road-racing bikes feel very stiff, with all effort going into moving the bike forward. Most road races are

Above: Brake levers on a racing bike combine brakes and gear-changing functions at the same place.

Above: Brakes on a racing bike are light, but strong, making it easy to control your speed on a fast descent.

Above: Modern racing bikes have as many as 11 sprockets on the rear wheel, giving a total of 22 gears so that riders can travel at high speeds.

Above: Racing saddles are narrow, for improved aerodynamics. Choose a saddle that is comfortable for you by testing as many as possible.

shorter distance events, taking between 1 and 3 hours to complete, so that for this distance it is possible to sacrifice a little comfort for stiffness and responsiveness.

Tour de France riders, however, can sometimes spend as much as 6 hours at a time on a racing bike so for the long distances they ride, comfort is of paramount importance.

Choosing a Racing Bike

Which racing bike are you going to buy? You will probably want a bike that is light, fast and responsive but your choice should depend on your current ability, your potential ability, your ambitions and the depth of your wallet.

By choosing to buy a good quality racing bike, you are already demonstrating that you are serious about riding fast and racing. To help achieve your maximum potential, the better the bike you buy, the faster you will ride.

As a rule of thumb, you should always buy the best possible equipment that you can afford, without getting into the mindset that you cannot ride fast without it. By focusing too much on equipment you run the risk of relying too hard on it. Instead of working overtime to afford a titanium seatpin bolt, you might end up going faster by investing that time in training more effectively.

Matching components

It is important to buy a bike with a matching level of componentry and frame. If you spend all your budget on a professional level frame, and only have

Right: Buy the racing bike that best suits your needs and level at the time.
Below: Carbon fibre is one of the lightest and strongest materials for making racing frames.

Carbon fibre or aluminium?

Bicycle technology has reached a point where there is so much choice that nearly everybody can find a racing frame that suits his or her needs and abilities perfectly. Deciding between carbon fibre and aluminium can, however, prove to be a difficult choice. Both are light, corrosion resistant and strong. Both give a stiff, responsive ride. The best way to choose is to test ride a model made in each material and see which you prefer.

Some people believe that a full-carbon frame tends toward a harsh ride. A good compromise is an aluminium frame that has carbon forks and seat stays.

Positioning

With compact frames available in three different sizes, it is easy to judge which one suits you. What is more important is to set up a comfortable and efficient riding position. The two most important measurements are saddle height and reach. There are several ways to determine the correct saddle height. Former Tour de France winner Greg Lemond recommends multiplying the distance between your crotch and the floor by 0.833. To do this, stand with your feet flat on the floor at the same distance apart as they would be on your bike, and keep your legs straight. Have a friend measure the distance for you.

Multiply this length by 0.833, and you have the correct figure for the distance between the centre of the bottom bracket and the saddle.

Your handlebars should be about 3cm (1¼in) below the level of your saddle. For greater aerodynamics, your handlebars can be a little lower, but this will come at the sacrifice of comfort.

When sitting on the saddle and holding the drops, your nose should be about 2cm (¾in) behind the horizontal part of the handlebar.

You can make micro-adjustments in your position, which will give you a more comfortable and efficient riding experience. When your pedals are at the same height, the front of your forward knee should be vertically above the central line of the axle of your pedal. Move your saddle back or forward a little to ensure that this is the case. If you have to do this, you may have to tweak your saddle height and stem, to ensure that all the angles are correct.

If you have long thighs, or a longer upper body, all this has to be taken into account when choosing your frame and setting up position.

enough left for a cheap groupset (the brakes, gears and drivetrain), there will be a compromise in performance.

For high-level racing, most riders choose between Shimano and Campagnolo groupsets. Shimano Dura Ace and Campagnolo Record are the

Above: Check that the distance from the saddle to the pedals is correct for you. Right: When setting up your bike, make sure that the reach is set at the correct distance for your size.

top range, and are highly engineered and reliable. As with choosing between carbon fibre and aluminium frames, the performance of both is so good that selecting one over the other is a matter of preference. The gear-changing system is different, and Campagnolo offers a more definite 'click' in between gears.

Wheels should have hubs compatible with the gearing system, and light, good quality rims. Advances in design, materials and spoke patterns ensure that there is a wide choice. For top level racing, a deep-section carbon rim is the best, but these are very expensive.

Left: An aluminium road and mountain bike frame is preferred by some riders.

Road-racing Skills: Breaking Away

Winning road races isn't easy. You share the start line with 150 other riders, who all want to win. Some are great climbers and others are great bunch sprinters. In a hilly race, if you are a good climber or a sprinter, you should make the most of these skills.

If you do not excel at sprinting or climbing, try to get into a breakaway. It's a rare road race in which the entire field rides round and waits for a group to sprint together (the bunch sprint). Attacks often go from the gun, and it takes special circumstances for the attack to be the right one.

Leading the charge
Attacking is energy-consuming. It is better to attack once, successfully, than four times unsuccessfully. The energy consumed in four unsuccessful attacks could make you miss the fifth, which is the one that disappears up the road. On the other hand, it might take those four attacks to succeed – the bunch may tire of chasing you down and let you go. Each race is different in this respect. But don't ever attack just for the sake of it. Choose your moment.

The best times to go are when the bunch slows down, either due to a corner, a hill, the fact that another group has just been chased down, or simply because the riders at the front stop riding hard. When you notice this happen, go as hard as you can. You may escape on your own, you may be followed by a small group in counterattack, or you may get chased down. After a few minutes, turn around and see which of these has happened. If you are on your own, but can see a small group working together to catch you 20 seconds behind, while the bunch is at a minute farther back, you are better off waiting for the small group to catch you. The short-term sacrifice of a handful of seconds is worth the long-

Right: The joy of victory – get it right and the win is yours.

Above: In a race, getting into the right breakaway is a crucial tactical skill.

term gain of being in the breakaway group and getting farther from the bunch than you could on your own. Be careful of who joins you, however. If the best sprinter in the race has made the bridge, there is little point in working well together – you might want to sit up and wait for the bunch to catch you. It may be a waste of energy, but so is towing a superior sprinter to the line, unless you are confident you can drop them before the finishing straight.

If you see somebody else attacking, your reaction must be fast. Every moment of hesitation means that there is a bigger gap to cross. When you see the telltale sign of a rider lifting themselves out of the saddle, try and make it a reflex to do exactly the same and put yourself right in their slipstream.

Individual riders often get away, but the most common breakaway is a small group, of between three and ten riders. Initially, these groups tend to work hard together to ensure that they are building a healthy lead over the pack.

You also need to know what the bunch are doing behind you. If they start chasing harder, it is worth marshalling the group to ride especially hard for 10–15km (6–9 miles). It's harder work, but if you can keep the gap at a constant level the bunch may become demoralized and back off. You will be more tired, but when the bunch slows, you can too.

Playing the field

Once groups have a minute or two of lead, riders work together, either by putting the lead at risk, or letting one or more riders do less work than the others. These riders will be fresher at the finish. There may be two riders from one team in the group. It may be your team. If there's a good sprinter in the group, you will need to get rid of them before the end. If you have superior numbers from your team, you can start to dictate things. If you or your team-mate is a good sprinter, it's worth the other rider sacrificing their chances in order to chase down attacks, lead the group at a fast pace to prevent attacks, and to do more of the work in order for the

Above: Solo breakaways are the hardest way to win, but the most spectacular.

sprinter to stay fresher. Or you can take turns in attacking, forcing the other riders to chase you down. If you attack enough times between you, it's a matter of time before an attack is successful.

Up against these tactics, you have to ride cleverly. If you are isolated you will have fewer opportunities to make an effort, but when you do, make sure it is the successful move. If another rider is pulling their team-mate to a sprint victory, make sure they are doing all the work and tiring themselves out, then launch a surprise attack near the finish. When two team-mates are attacking in turn, allow others to chase them down the first time at least. When the second or third attack happens, react at once, get into their slipstream and wait. If you are away, you now have a 50 per cent chance of winning. If you get chased down, go with the counterattack from the other team-mate.

In a breakaway situation, your main aims are working hard to ensure the break stays away, then using as little energy as possible when the tactical games start. Relax, watch your breakaway companions, and make your race-winning effort at just the right moment.

Left: Share the work with your breakaway companions, but be careful to watch them all the time.

Road-racing Skills: Climbing

Climbing is the hardest part of bike racing. Even good climbers suffer when they ride uphill, while for bad climbers, hills can be the difference between winning and losing a race. It is important to know how to climb.

A strategically placed hill can blow a race apart, so you need to know how to deal with them in a race.

Some people are born climbers. They are generally light, skinny and small, with a large power-to-weight ratio. For these lucky people, hills are where they can really put pressure on the rest of the field. If they also have good technique and tactical sense, they are very hard to deal with in a race.

Others don't climb so well. Larger, heavier riders have more weight to carry up the hills. Others find it difficult to react to changes in pace on uphills. However, even poor climbers can greatly improve their performance by using the best tactics in each situation.

In a race, whether you are a good climber or bad climber, it is important to be at the front when the climb starts. Poor climbers hope that by doing this, they can slip back through the bunch, and still be in contact as the race passes over the top. If these riders start the hill at the back, that is where they will stay. Good climbers need to follow the same tactic, so that they are in position to

dictate the race or react to others trying to do so. It can take several kilometres of racing to get to the front in time for the bottom, so be prepared.

Hitting your stride

On a long climb, cadence and rhythm are important. Pushing a big gear slowly is an expensive way of riding, and increases the chances that you will tire before the top. The best way of riding is to train yourself to ride in a much lower gear. This gives your legs greater 'snap' when making or reacting to an attack.

Breathing is difficult when climbing, so when climbing sitting down, try and sit more upright, holding the tops of the handlebars, thereby opening up the chest. Sometimes, when the speed

Left: Climbing in a race can be intense and painful – always maintain focus, as this rider is doing here.

Above: The easiest way around a hairpin bend is towards the middle of the road. Follow this line and you could save crucial energy for later on.

increases, or just to stay on top of the gear, you will need to stand up. A good climber can vary their position and rhythm between seated and standing climbing – train yourself to do this so that when you need to do it in a race you are ready.

The best line to follow through the corners on a climb is not necessarily the shortest one. Road corners are often much steeper on the inside than the outside, which could force you to work harder than you need to to maintain your speed. The most advantageous way is halfway between the two sides of the road, unless the corner is really steep, in which case it might be more efficient to move out farther. The important thing is

Left: If you are a good climber, attacking uphill can put dangerous rivals out of contention.

If they increase the pace slowly, go with it. It is going to hurt, but you will be maintaining a rhythm, which is more straightforward than responding to varying pace. If they attack suddenly, don't attempt to follow them, as you would an attack on the flat. Remain calm, and slowly increase the pace. Unless they are in super shape, an attack by a climber will be followed by a deceleration. Accelerate slowly to the point where you can bring them back. By catching them, you can make them doubt their ability to get away. If a climber is varying the pace, try to ignore them and ride at your own rhythm.

When climbing gets really painful, it can help to use mental techniques to master the pain. Counting to 10 over and over again will help you focus through the pain. If the climb is a long

to conserve as much energy as possible, and spinning through the less steep part of a corner enables you to do this.

What is necessary while climbing, for good and bad climbers alike, is having the self-knowledge to know your limits and how you react to riding at certain speeds, and to be able to focus through periods of great discomfort. Train yourself in both of these, and your climbing will improve.

Left: If you get attacked on a climb, respond, and it may help to discourage further attacks.

Tactics for a good climber

The best climbers use three methods to make life exceedingly miserable for everybody else in a race. The first is the most straightforward and involves going to the front and gradually accelerating until they are riding as fast as they can. Hanging on to them in this kind of situation is difficult.

The second is by attacking hard, and quickly accelerating away. The third method is, perversely, slowing down. Climbers can deal with changes in rhythm much better than non-climbers can, and by slowing things down they are making the other riders vulnerable to attacks.

If you are a good climber, practise all these methods and try to use them to your advantage.

Tactics for a bad climber

Bad climbers will have to come up with ways of preventing good climbers from putting them to the back of a race. By training hard and being confident of your tactics you may be able to neutralize good climbers.

Above: On long, steady climbs, stay as relaxed and focused as possible and hold your pace.

one, focus on getting to the next bend. Break the climb into smaller sections, which are mentally easier to deal with.

Bad climbers are especially vulnerable on races with hilltop finishes. There is no way you can hope to compete with a good climber here. Instead, you should work on getting into a break, giving you a head start.

Road-racing Skills: Cornering and Descending

Taking a corner fast, either on the flat or riding downhill, takes skill, balance and confidence. Deficiencies in any of these areas can lead to a rider being dropped. All these skills are easy to work on, and can be used to advantage in a race.

Your bike can only lean over through a corner so far before one of two things happens. Either your pedal will scrape the floor (if you are pedalling), with dire consequences, or your tyres' traction will be lost, which would be equally catastrophic. On a gravelly surface, this can happen at a very slight angle.

Dealing with a corner in a bike race involves three phases. First comes the approach, during which you adjust your speed to the level necessary to go through the corner. Next is the apex, which is the sharpest part of the corner. And finally there is the exit, which is where you can accelerate out again.

Cornering

In a bunch, the first rider will choose the racing line around the corner, generally swinging out in the approach, then turning their wheel and passing close to the apex. Finally they will swing out again as they accelerate away. If the bunch is strung out in a single line, follow the rider ahead, using the same line, trying to lose as little speed as possible. Do not attempt to overtake on the inside, where you are vulnerable to crashing and also disrupting the flow of the line of riders. By cutting up the inside, you are effectively moving into the racing line of other riders as they cut into the apex, which will make you unpopular. If riders are bunched up, follow close to the racing line and adjust your speed to match the riders around you.

When going around the apex, keep the outside leg down, and lean your bike, while keeping your head upright, to maintain the maximum speed possible. The idea is to cut from the outside of the road to the inside through the apex, then swing wide again once you have passed it. As soon as your bike

stops swinging wide, you have entered the exit phase and are ready to start pedalling again.

In a race, you can make others work harder through corners by getting to the front, keeping the speed high, and then accelerating hard out of the corner. This has the effect of stretching out the bunch, and riders have to work hard to close gaps that have opened up. Repeat this a few times, and your rivals may not have the energy to chase an attack.

Above: Descending fast and safely is an essential skill in bike racing – getting the racing line right is crucial.

Some bike races are flat, but most include hills for the sake of variety and to add a challenge. Going up the hill is not the only challenge – bunches race fast down the other side, and this is where less confident descenders get found out.

If your race is taking place on open roads, your first priority should always be safety in the case of meeting cars or

Cornering on the flat

Approach: *During the approach, adjust your speed to go around the corner.*

Apex: *The sharpest part of the corner is the apex. Lean into it as you go around.*

Exit: *The exit is the final part of the corner where you begin accelerating out.*

other traffic. Stay on the correct side of the road in case there is a car around a blind corner. The same warning applies for training rides.

Descending
The first rule of descending is to keep your head up, look ahead and anticipate what is going to happen in front of you. Unless you are leading the bunch, you may have to react to the movements of other riders. Effective descending means having a comfortable and aerodynamic position on the bike. Always hold the drops of your handlebars, with one or two fingers on the brake levers, so you can react fast to obstacles. Keep your

centre of gravity low, for better balance and aerodynamics. If you can see a long way ahead, you can go into a tuck position, with your hands on the tops of the handlebars and your chin almost touching your wrists. Use your legs as shock absorbers by putting more of your weight on the pedals and sitting on the tip of your saddle.

It is important to corner well going downhill. Slow down before a corner, to a speed that will allow you to go around the bend without crashing. If you are in a bunch, don't make sudden movements if you want to change your position, but do signal your intentions clearly in case somebody is trying to get around you.

Above: To enter a bend, swing wide, then cut in to the apex of the curve.

Cornering on a descent

Approach: *To begin, swing wide, and accelerate towards the corner.*

Apex: *Follow a natural line, stay relaxed and look forward with head up.*

Exit: *Start pedalling as you hit the exit with the bike starting to straighten.*

Road-racing Skills: Sprinting

Sprinters win far more bike races than any other kind of bike rider. They have the advantage of being able to wait until the finishing line is in sight and then unleashing their primary weapon. Various tactics can be employed to win the day.

Field sprinting demands nerve, speed, strength, determination and timing. When a rider has all of these attributes, he or she is very difficult to beat.

Sprinting, at a basic level, involves riding as fast as possible over a short distance, but there is more than one way of doing this.

Some sprints are won by a rider jumping to the front early in the race and holding their speed all the way to the line. Others are won by a rider getting into the slipstream of the rider who has made the early jump, taking advantage of the wind protection offered by their rival, then overtaking them in the final 50m (164ft).

Strength or speed?

Some riders rely on sheer brute strength in their sprint. If they can turn a bigger gear than anybody else, they can go the fastest. These riders favour a long, drawn-out sprint. Riders at the opposite end of the sprinting scale rely on leg speed. They don't need to use as high a gear as the power sprinters, but instead turn a smaller gear faster. The advantage of this method is that their acceleration is far quicker, enabling them to speed away from other riders very quickly.

In a race, the preparation for a sprint starts as far as 20km (12.5 miles) from the finishing line. If you want to be involved in the sprint you need to make sure you are riding near the front well before the finish. Take time to move up the bunch, staying out of the wind as much as possible. Ideally, you will have a team-mate or two to help you do this.

In the Tour de France, the sprinters' teams maintain a very high speed at the front of the bunch for the final 10km (6 miles), to discourage breakaways from spoiling their leader's chance of a win. In smaller races, the run-in tends to be more of a free-for-all. Stay near the front without going into the lead, so you can watch the way the race is developing.

Jockeying for position

With 3km (1.8 miles) to go, the real manoeuvring starts. Riding behind another rider saves energy, so the sprinters bump and barge each other to defend their position behind another rider. If there is a strong sprinter in the field, other riders keep close to their wheel, following them in the sprint and jumping around them to steal the win. There is only one place on his wheel, even if four or five riders are fighting for it.

As the race enters the final 500m (1,640ft), the riders start to fan across the road as the sprint is launched. Although every sprint is different, you should be aiming to start your final sprint with about 200m (656ft) to go. Try to stay on another sprinter's wheel until this point. Accelerate hard at this point and spend the next 50m (164ft) building up to speed. Then try to hold your top speed all the way to the finishing line.

Phases of sprinting

Acceleration and speed maintenance are the two phases of sprinting. Acceleration has to be a sudden increase in speed to reach top speed as fast as possible, to get around riders in front of you, and to shake off riders who are on your wheel. If gear selection is too high, it will take too long to accelerate; too low, and you will not be able to reach top speed. Terrain and wind direction must be taken into consideration. Grip the drops of the handlebars firmly, stand up on the pedals and jump as hard as you

Left: Bike races are often decided with a fast and furious bunch sprint. Good tactics make all the difference in a sprint.

How to sprint

1: *To sprint, jump hard, holding the handlebars firmly.*

2: *Push down with one leg; pull up handlebars with the opposite hand.*

3: *When you reach maximum speed, maintain it as long as you can.*

4: *Bend your arms. Use the upper body to best effect.*

5: *Extend arms and legs to push the bike over the line.*

can, putting as much force through the pedal stroke as you can, again and again. Use your upper body and each arm in turn to pull the handlebars up as you push down on the pedal with the opposite foot. Initially your acceleration will be slow, but as momentum builds up, you can get towards your top speed.

Finishing the sprint

Once you hit top speed, your aim is to maintain it to the finishing line. If you start to slow, other riders who have timed their sprint better will come past you. Keep your eyes forward, ignore other riders, and maintain a straight line to the finishing line to avoid obstructing other riders, for which you can be disqualified.

It is also the shortest distance. Don't slow in the final metres, even if you think you have won, but pedal hard through the finishing line, with the final strong thrust of the pedals coinciding with straightening your arms to 'push' your bike ahead. This is called 'throwing' the bike, and it can be the crucial skill that gains you victory.

Road-racing Skills: Strategies and Teamwork

It is often said that cycling is a team sport for individuals, and it is true that only one rider can win the race. However, that victory may well be partly due to the sacrifice and hard work of the rider's team-mates.

Getting into the right position in a race involves thorough pre-race planning, and clever decision-making during a race. Team tactics must be well thought out and flexible enough to allow unpredictable events to be dealt with.

Before the race

The most important part of preparation for a race is to train properly for the weeks and months leading up to it. Turning up at a race unfit is a waste of your time. If the race is an important one, ease off your training in the run-up to it, so that you are in tip-top condition on the morning of the event.

Well before the race, you should research its route. Knowledge of the roads you are racing on is a huge advantage. If the race is local, you can train on the route, get used to the corners, decide which gears you need to use, find out where the course might be exposed to crosswinds, and notice subtle variations in the gradient of the finishing straight. All of this information is a powerful tool in riding a good race.

Knowing that there is a hill might not be good enough. You need to know if it is steep at the bottom, or steep at the top. Is there a descent straight away, or does it emerge on to a plateau, which will be windy and could split the bunch up even more than the climb? Is there a sharp corner just at the bottom of the climb? If so, going around it in first position will enable you to accelerate and gain distance on your rivals, who will have to work hard to chase you down. Does your race finish on a hill,

Above: Lance Armstrong was helped to seven Tour de France wins by his US Postal and Discovery Channel teams.

and if so, who is your team's best climber? Is there a sharp corner 400m (1,312ft) before the finishing line? No detail is too small to help in your preparation. By knowing the course, you can also train specifically for its challenges, which will stand you in good physical stead.

Know your enemy

The course is one area that you should research well before the race; another is your rivals. They want to win the race as badly as you do, and they have their own plans for doing so. Good climbers need to be neutralized during the flat part of the course. Good sprinters need

Left: Researching the route and working out strategies with team-mates ahead of the race can give a team an advantage.

to be kept to the back in the hills. If there is a particularly strong team taking part, rather than trying to beat them single-handedly, it might be better to apply the old saying, 'if you can't beat them, join them.'

Try to get into breaks with their riders and work with them, which effectively makes them, and the riders they have in the bunch, your temporary team-mates. You can work out how to beat them once you have carved up the race between you.

Lastly, look at the weather forecast the day before the race and bring the correct riding clothes for the conditions.

During the race

You should have formulated 'Plan A' before the race. This might involve getting a specific rider in your team away in an early attack on the first climb of the race. Or it could involve waiting for the finishing sprint.

Because these plans are fairly inflexible, and could be compromised by the actions of other riders in the race, you also have to react well to the prevailing circumstances. You might designate one or two riders who are under instructions to make sure that at least one of them is in every early break. This takes the pressure off the rest of your team to chase breaks down.

If you find yourself with a team-mate farther up the road in a break, your job is twofold. First, there is no need to expend energy in chasing down the break – you can leave this to others. Second, you should be vigilant for counterattacks, which might put your

Above: If you are a strong climber, use hills to get ahead during a race.

escaped team-mate in a weaker position. If counterattacks happen, it's worth trying to get another team-mate into them. If the tables are turned and your team has missed the break, it will be your responsibility, along with other teams who missed the break, to chase it down. If this is the case, don't use the whole team to ride as hard as possible on the front, or you will all be burned out by the finish. Instead, try and share the work with another team, using just a couple of riders to up the pace gradually and eat into the break's lead.

Apart from these strategies, the main aim of the race is to expend as little energy as possible so that you are still strong at the end. Stay close behind other riders as much as is practical. Don't panic as events unfold, but react to them calmly.

Left: By sheltering their leader (in the middle) from the wind, team-mates help him to save vital energy in a race.

Road-racing Skills: Time Trialling

The ability to time trial is one of the most important skills in cycling. Being able to ride fast and maintain a fast pace is a necessity not only in time trialling but also in road racing, when you are in an escape, or when chasing down a break.

Time trialling involves riding at a steady and consistent rate. The aim is never to ride so fast that you are unable to maintain your pace, and not to slow down – a feat which requires concentration, nerve, resistance to pain, endurance and strength.

Some riders are naturally better at time trialling than others. It is also a trainable skill. By working hard on your body position and endurance, and practising a lot, you can bring about improvements in your time-trialling results.

Time trials can be individual races, or part of a stage race. In the latter, you can afford to lose a little time if you know you can gain time in another stage. In an individual race, the fastest man or woman wins. It involves getting up to speed quickly and steadily, then maintaining the effort until the finish.

Your starting effort in a time trial should not be the same as an attack in a road race, or a jump in a sprint. Instead, accelerate gradually so that you don't overwork your muscles. At the same time, don't relax too much at this point – you need to be at cruising speed sooner rather than later.

Pacing yourself

Finding out what pace you can sustain over a long time trial involves training with a pulse monitor and working out

the percentage of your maximum heart rate you can ride at without becoming exhausted. This takes experimentation. Maintaining this pace should not be a comfortable process. During a time trial, your body will be in a great deal of pain, and you need to focus through this and be confident that you can maintain the same level of effort.

Riding at the same pace during a race is often made difficult by corners, hills and weather conditions. Some riders make the mistake of trying to maintain speed up hills and into a headwind; the extra effort will make them collapse later. The effort should be the constant, not the speed. There is no need to panic if it feels like you are riding slowly – your rivals will be doing the same. As with road races, knowing the course will

Left: Time-trial bikes need fewer gears than road bikes, especially on the flat. Right: Time-trial bikes handle less well than road bikes, so you have to take care to avoid crashes.

Top: Good time trialling requires a bike with solid disc wheels, which are more aerodynamic than spoked wheels.

assist in planning your race. If you have paced yourself correctly, you should be feeling weary in the second half of the course. This is the time to hold your nerve and focus. If possible add a little extra effort, without crossing into the red zone, ensuring that by the finishing line you are at your peak output.

Time-trialling bikes

Road-racing bikes and time-trialling bikes are different. Aerodynamics are important for time-trialling bikes, since the speed will be greater than in other kinds of race. The bike is narrow, and puts the rider in a position in which the arms are ahead of the body, the back and head are as low as possible, while still letting the legs turn at maximum capacity.

Frames are stiffer than for bikes for road-racing. The greater distances in road racing mean that stiffness has to be balanced against comfort. Time trials tend to be shorter and comfort is not so important. By making the frame stiffer, less power is lost by the frame flexing, resulting in a faster ride.

Above: Time-trialling handlebars are arranged so that they put the arms and body into an aerodynamic tuck, with the head and back in a low position.

Anatomy of a time-trial bike

❶ Rear wheel: The wheels can be spoked or a solid disc.

❷ Front wheel: Deep rims cut down on the length of the spokes, which are flat, to reduce drag.

❸ Frame: Moulded carbon fibre frame with flatter tubes. Extremely stiff, at the expense of long-distance comfort.

❹ Handlebars: Special low-profile 'tri-bars' allow the rider to rest on their elbows with the arms stretched out ahead, giving a far more aerodynamic profile.

❺ Chainrings: 53–44 or even less discrepancy in size, unless the bike is to be used on a very hilly course.

❻ Sprockets: 8- or 9-speed freewheel with 12–19 or 12–21 block.

❼ Gear-changers: These are mounted on the end of the tri-bars for ease of access.

❽ Clothing: One-piece tight-fitting skinsuits and profiled helmets catch less wind than regular cycling clothing.

Racing Skills: Triathlon

Triathlons involve sandwiching a bike race between a swim and a run. For many cyclists, they are an activity that present an extra challenge, and also lead to greater all-round fitness. The training discipline for a triathlon is very similar to that for cycling.

Triathlons are almost a pure endurance sport, in which judgement of pace and resistance to fatigue are the most important skills. The three sports are difficult enough on their own, but together they form a unique challenge.

When cyclists start triathlon training, the greatest challenge is forcing the body to work with different muscle groups. When making the transition, it is recommended that you spend a few months just getting used to swimming and running without going into any structured training routines.

Once your body is used to working in these different ways, it is a good idea to work with a swimming coach, who will improve your technique. The typical swim for an Olympic-distance triathlon is 1,500m (approximately 1 mile) – bad technique over this distance will slow you down and tire you out, and good cycling may not be enough to compensate. Better technique will greatly improve your swimming times.

If you are an experienced cyclist going into triathlons, work on maintaining your cycling economy and fitness – this

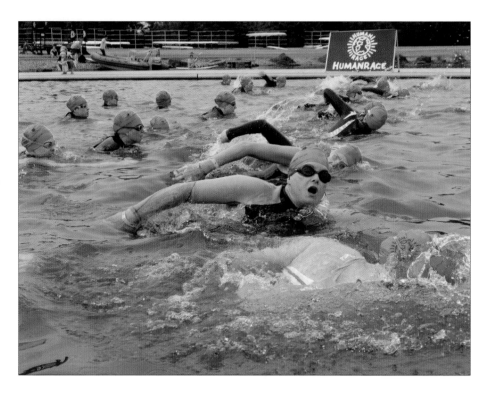

Above: Triathlons often begin with a massed start swim in which positioning is a crucial factor.
Below: Experienced cyclists have an advantage over their competitors in the bike leg of a triathlon.

Triathlon bike

At first glance, a typical triathlon bike looks very similar to a time-trial bike. However, the special nature of the exertion in the course of a triathlon means that the athletes have some needs not shared by time triallists.

First, the position of a triathlete is not as low down as a time triallist. The saddle should remain at the optimum height for maximum performance, but the handlebars should be raised so that the position is not so extreme. The bike section of a triathlon is followed by a run, which puts strain on the hamstrings. If the triathlete uses a low position, he or she risks injury during the run.

Second, there are two water bottles carried on the frame. The athlete will not have had a chance to rehydrate during the swimming leg. The bike is a good time to refuel and ensure consumption of enough energy to get through the run. Both bottles will probably be necessary.

is the part of the race in which you will have an advantage over swimmers who are starting the bike stage ahead of you.

The running stage is an unusual kind of exertion. Although running training is absolutely necessary, you also need to train yourself to run after a long bike ride. Your body is tired by now and this will slow down your running, so, as well as swimming, cycling and running training, you also need to incorporate what are known as 'brick' sessions into your training routine. These involve a training session linking two of the disciplines, most often cycling and running. A typical brick session might involve a 30-minute warm-up followed by 10-minute sets alternating between the bike (on a stationary trainer, unless you have an exact training route) and running. Cycle at 75 to 80 per cent of MHR for 10 minutes, then run at the same intensity for 10 minutes. Then repeat, before warming down. These sessions are essential if you are to achieve your potential in a triathlon.

Quick changes

The other challenge facing triathletes is to 'transition' as quickly and efficiently as possible between the three stages.

Right: Save time in the transition zone by having your equipment prepared exactly as you want it.

Above: The run leg of a triathlon is extremely arduous because of the fatigue after the swim and bike legs.

This is complicated by the fact that competitors often wear a wetsuit for the swim (if it is in cold, open water), and need to change shoes for both the cycle and the run. Organization and relaxed focus is necessary to do this as quickly as possible. When you leave the water, start to unzip your wetsuit as you jog towards the bike pen. Take your wetsuit off carefully but fast, so your feet don't get caught, then run with your bike

Above: During the transition time, take the opportunity to refocus on the next discipline.

(with shoes attached to pedals) out of the bike pen to the start of the bike leg. Mount the bike and put your feet into your shoes as you move off.

For the next transition, take your feet out of your shoes at the end of the ride and dismount the bike, running to the pen. Get your running shoes on as quickly as possible, and you are set. Transitions are an easy process, but rushing can add minutes to your finish time.

Great Road Races: The Tour de France

The Tour de France is the greatest race in cycling history. Because it is the first and oldest of the Grand Tours, with the best slot on the cycling calendar in mid-July and terrain perfectly suited to bike racing, it captures the imagination of the cycling world each summer.

The Tour is a stage race. The approximately 3,000km (1,865-mile) route is divided into daily stages, generally between 150 and 250km (93–155 miles), with time trials on some days. The riders start each stage together, and their accumulated time is added into the general classification.

Yellow jersey

The leader of the general classification wears a yellow jersey. There is also a points classification, for the rider who consistently gets the best stage placings, and a red and white dotted jersey for the best climber, known as the King of the Mountains. The yellow jersey is that colour because the original sponsoring newspaper, *L'Auto*, was printed on yellow paper. In the early years of the race it was pointed out that nobody knew who was winning the race, and the tradition of handing them a yellow jersey at the end of each stage was born.

Test of strength

The race is extremely arduous, with only two rest days during the three weeks. The route is different every year and in recent times has followed a clockwise direction one year and the next year, an anticlockwise direction.

The race always spends five or six days in the high mountains, crossing the Alps and Pyrenees. Riders can lose huge amounts of time in these stages, and many are forced to pull out.

In some years, when the organizers want to make the event particularly tough, the race goes into the Massif Central mountain range in central France for a day or two. The race has a different start – known as 'Le Grand Départ' – every year, but always finishes with a well deserved celebration stage on the Champs Elysées in Paris.

Above: Fans flock to the Tour de France in their thousands every summer, hoping for a glimpse of their cycling heroes.

1952

The most impressive Tours are the closest ones, and those that are dominated by a single rider. The year 1952 saw an Italian climber at the peak of his powers, with his rivals simply unable to keep up with him.

Fausto Coppi probably would have won whatever the route in 1952, but the organizers blessed him with a mountainous route including the first-ever summit finishes – three of them, at Puy de Dôme, Alpe d'Huez and Sestrières. He won each of these stages, as well as a long time trial early in the race. Journalists, with very little to write about in the way of a close race (second-placed Stan Ockers was at least 28 minutes behind, which was a massive margin), waxed lyrical about Coppi's win, seeing it as nothing short of legendary.

Below: Fausto Coppi was one of the first heroes of the modern era, winning the Tour de France three times in the 1950s.

Above: Frenchman Jacques Anquetil, who was the first man to win the Tour de France five times.

Above: Eddy Merckx, who won five Tours in dominant style during the 1960s and 1970s.

Above: Greg Lemond time trials his way to victory in the 1989 Tour de France, the closest race ever.

1964

In 1964, the race was a battle between two Frenchmen – four-times winner Jacques Anquetil and his great rival Raymond Poulidor. Anquetil was the more successful on the bike, while Poulidor was more popular with fans.

In 1964, Poulidor came very close to toppling Anquetil. On the climb of the Puy de Dôme, the two rode side by side, elbows clashing, weaving up the road as they fought to win. Unbeknown to Poulidor, Anquetil was feeling terrible, but he bluffed his way up, fighting the agony to stay with Poulidor. Poulidor only realized too late that Anquetil was vulnerable and he attacked with sufficient time to drop Anquetil, but not enough to take the yellow jersey, which Anquetil eventually won by 55 seconds.

1969

As in 1952, 1969 saw a single rider dominate the race. His name was Eddy Merckx, and he was about to take the first of his five Tour de France victories. His nickname was the 'Cannibal', which referred to his voracious appetite for winning races and destroying the opposition. In 1969 the 24-year-old Belgian was unrivalled. He took the yellow jersey as the race entered the Alps in the first week, and held it to the finish. He took a brilliant solo victory on the 17th stage in the Pyrenees, attacking early and spending the day on his own at the front. He won by almost 20 minutes.

1989

This was simply the most dramatic race in Tour history. The excitement started when defending champion Pedro Delgado turned up late for the first stage and lost almost 3 minutes before he had began turning the pedals. The lead swung between Greg Lemond, on the comeback after a hunting accident, and two-times winner Laurent Fignon through the flat first week and the Pyrenees. Delgado began to claw his way back into contention.

In the Alps, Fignon looked the stronger, and two attacks on successive days put him 50 seconds into the lead with only a 30km time trial into Paris to go. Lemond beat him by 58 seconds, gaining the yellow jersey by 8 seconds.

2003

Lance Armstrong had dominated the race for four years previously, but in 2003 he almost failed. He was unable to stamp his authority on the race in his usual style, and although he wore the yellow jersey through the Alps and Pyrenees, his lead was slim, and he looked vulnerable to the attacks made by his rivals. He took a beating in a long time trial. On one day, one of his closest rivals, Joseba Beloki, fell off directly in front of Armstrong on a steep corner in the Alps. Armstrong was forced to take spectacular evasive action, and ended up riding across a field, jumping off his bike and carrying it back on to the road. In

the Pyrenees, his handlebar got caught on a spectator's bag strap, pulling him off his bike. He still managed to put in a race-winning attack farther up the road, defending a slim lead in the final time trial.

2008

The Tour in 2008 was one of the most tactical and closest ever. There were no outstanding favourites, and with only days left to race, there were still six riders within a minute of the lead, an unprecedented situation. In the Alps, in the last week, Spanish rider Carlos Sastre made an all-or-nothing attack on the Alpe d'Huez climb, and gained enough time to win the Tour.

Below: Lance Armstrong, the absolute record holder in the Tour, with seven wins.

10 Best-ever Tour de France Riders

The Tour de France is one of the most important stage races for cycling aficionados. It is a tough race, taking around 23 days and covering more than 3,000 kilometres (1,865 miles). To be the best, riders need endurance and great physical strength.

1) Lance Armstrong (USA)
TOUR WINS: SEVEN

Armstrong dominated the Tour de France between 1999 and 2005. He won seven on the trot, and in six of these he was unchallengeable. The exception was 2003, when he started tired, and struggled all the way to victory only 1 minute ahead of German rival Jan Ullrich.

2) Eddy Merckx (Belgium)
TOUR WINS: FIVE

Merckx won five Tours between 1969 and 1974, as well as virtually every other race on the calendar. His insatiable appetite for succeeding ensured that he won more stages than any other rider and spent more days in the yellow jersey than anyone else.

3) Bernard Hinault (France)
TOUR WINS: FIVE

The last indomitable French winner of the Tour de France took his fifth title in 1985. Hinault had an aggressive, confrontational style, in life as in racing, and didn't suffer fools gladly.

4) Miguel Indurain (Spain)
TOUR WINS: FIVE

Indurain was the first rider to win five successive Tours, between 1991 and 1995. He was an awesome time triallist, building a big lead in the individual tests, and hanging on to the best climbers in the mountains.

5) Jacques Anquetil (France)

TOUR WINS: FIVE

Anquetil was the first rider to win five Tours, taking his first in 1957, then another four between 1961 and 1964. His career was defined by his great rivalry with the more popular Raymond Poulidor, whose nickname 'the eternal second' revealed which of the two riders was faster on the bike.

6) Greg Lemond (USA)

TOUR WINS: THREE

Lemond was the first American rider to win the Tour de France. His career was interrupted by a hunting accident in which he nearly lost his life. On recovering, he showed his ability in an amazing comeback, and stormed through to win the 1989 race by only 8 seconds, which was the closest race in history.

7) Louison Bobet (France)

TOUR WINS: THREE

Bobet won three successive Tours between 1951 and 1953, starting a golden age in French cycling. Including his wins, French riders won 11 out of 15 Tours, a record they have rarely approached since. His performance in the 1953 Tour was considered to be one of the finest ever because the conditions were so difficult.

8) Philippe Thys (Belgium)

TOUR WINS: THREE

The first triple winner of the race, Thys would probably have won a lot more Tours if his career had not been interrupted by World War I. Although he started off as a cyclo-cross champion, he went on to win the Tour de France in 1913, 1914 and 1920. He won five stages in 1922 and two stages in the tour of 1924.

9) Fausto Coppi (Italy)

TOUR WINS: TWO

As with Thys, war took Coppi's best racing years from him and his racing career took place when travelling across borders was not particularly easy. He dominated the Tour in the mountains in a way rarely seen in the history of the race. His 1952 win has been described as the best Tour de France victory.

10) Laurent Fignon (France)

TOUR WINS: TWO

Fignon won the Tour at the age of 22 in 1983, and after thrashing Bernard Hinault the following year, it was expected that he would go on to win many more Tours. But plagued by injury, poor morale and a spate of bad luck, the rest of his career was blighted, and he missed out on winning in 1989 by just 8 seconds.

Great Road Races: The Giro d'Italia

The cycling season doesn't begin and end with the Tour de France. There are two other Grand Tours, the Tour of Italy and the Tour of Spain, as well as a whole host of stage races and one-day races from February through to October every year.

The Giro d'Italia, or Tour of Italy, is the first Grand Tour of the year, taking place in late May and early June. Like the Tour de France, it is three weeks long, and is contested in the same way, with daily stages and a general classification. The leader of the race wears a pink jersey, known as the 'maglia rosa', in the same way as the Tour de France leader wears a yellow jersey.

The race is as tough as the Tour de France, with stages in the Alps and Dolomite mountain ranges. In recent years, the Giro d'Italia organizers have tried to design ever-tougher mountain stages, to make it the hardest race in the world.

1949

Just like in the 1952 Tour de France, Fausto Coppi dominated the 1949 Giro with superb lone attacks in the mountains. His closest rival was Gino Bartali, who finished 24 minutes behind.

On a sporting level, it was a one-horse race, but the rivalry between Coppi and Bartali divided the nation. As Italy emerged from the chaos of World War II, it stood at a crossroads between the old ways, and the modern ways of the Western world. Bartali was a pious Catholic, who attracted the older, more conservative fans, while Coppi, divorced and conducting a public affair with another woman, represented the secular, modern world. The fans played out the cultural war using Coppi and Bartali as symbols of their beliefs.

1987

The 1987 Giro d'Italia was possibly the most entertaining Grand Tour of them all, with a bitter feud raging at the heart of the race. Irishman Stephen Roche was the winner. He took the lead midway through the race, with an attack on a mountain stage. That might not have been a problem in itself, except that he was riding for an Italian team, in Italy,

Below: The Irish cyclist, Stephen Roche, who won the 1987 Giro d'Italia.

Above: Andy Hampsten, winner of the 1988 Giro d'Italia. He won the race in terrible conditions in the mountains.

and the rider he relieved of the pink jersey was his Italian team-mate Roberto Visentini. It caused a scandal.

Visentini spent the rest of the race conducting a war of words in the press with Roche, who could no longer rely on the support of his team-mates. The crowds by the roadside yelled abuse and threw missiles at Roche as he rode past, while Visentini tried to knock him off his bike. Roche prevailed and went on to win a historic triple in the same year – the Giro, the Tour and the World Championships.

1988

After the drama of 1987, it was only a year before the next big drama in the race. On a mountain stage to Bormio, in the Dolomites, the weather took a turn for the worse. It was raining in the valleys, but the stage was going over the 2,600m (8,500ft) Gavia pass, where the rain turned to snow. In apocalyptic conditions, the organizers refused to stop the race, forcing riders to struggle up through

Above: Fausto Coppi, who became a hero for Italian fans by winning the Giro d'Italia five times in the 40s and 50s.

the blizzard, then, which was worse, ride down the other side. American Andy Hampsten and Dutchman Erik Breukink handled the conditions the best, putting almost 5 minutes between them and the next rider, and Hampsten went on to win the race.

Above: The 18th stage of the Vuelta a España in 2007.

The Vuelta a España

The Tour of Spain, known as the Vuelta a España, is the third Grand Tour of the cycling season. It is not as big or brash as its counterparts in Italy and France, and suffered from a crisis in confidence when it was moved from May, when it used to attract good quality international stars, to September, towards the end of a long and tiring season. It is said that there are two kinds of riders at the Vuelta – those who want to win the race, and those who have been sent there as punishment. The Vuelta is a three-week stage race and the route changes each year but usually includes steep climbs. Nevertheless, it is still an important race. Spain emerged as a powerful cycling nation in the late 1980s and 1990s. Pedro Delgado and Miguel Indurain's Tour de France wins brought more fans to the Vuelta.

Nobody has ever dominated the Vuelta like Merckx dominated the Giro and Armstrong dominated the Tour – the record for victories is three by Swiss rider Tony Rominger between 1992 and 1994, and even Merckx only managed to win it once. Indurain famously never managed to win it, claiming it came at a time of the season when allergies affected his form.

Great Road Races: The Classics

As well as the Grand Tours, there are also many one-day races throughout the cycling year. The biggest and oldest are the five major Classics held at venues in Europe. The only other one-day race that comes close in terms of prestige is the World Championships.

For many riders and fans, the five Classics and the World Championship races are the ultimate prize – even more important than the Tour de France. For each Classic, there is an outstanding race or a rider that fought against all the odds to win. These races will never be forgotten.

Milan–San Remo

Known as 'La Primavera', Milan–San Remo happens as spring reaches northern Italy. It is a mainly flat race, which attracts the bunch sprinters, but two strategically placed hills near the finish always have the potential to stir things up. The most memorable race took place in 1983. This race has a fond place in the hearts of Italian cycling fans. The home favourite, Giuseppe Saronni, was the winner. He was wearing the rainbow jersey of world champion, which simultaneously heaped the pressure on to his shoulders, and made his victory all the more worthwhile. He attacked alone on the Poggio, the final climb into San Remo, and held off the bunch on the descent to the finish line.

Tour of Flanders

The whole of Belgium stops what it is doing on the day of the Tour of Flanders. Belgian cycling fans are among the most passionate in the world, and if they get a home winner, the excitement is comparable with a national holiday.

The race includes several steep cobbled climbs, called 'bergs', and rutted, sometimes muddy tracks, where the atmosphere is second to none. The race is usually decided on the climbs.

Belgian cycling fell into something of a decline when Eddy Merckx retired in 1977. The country embarked on a fruitless search to replace their hero, whose ability and wins will probably never be equalled in the sport.

In 2005, however, a new national hero emerged in the form of sprinter Tom Boonen. He dominated the race, making his rivals look second-rate with a searing attack in the final 10km (6 miles).

Left: Andrei Tchmil wins the Paris–Roubaix, the best performance of modern times.
Right: Giuseppe Saronni, who won the unforgettable 1983 Milan–San Remo.

Above: Tom Boonen (left), the Belgian rider who won a famous Tour of Flanders in 2005.

Paris–Roubaix

Famous for the cobbled farm tracks that appear with increasing frequency in the second half of the race, Paris–Roubaix is a hard race to ride. The rough tracks turn the race into a war of attrition,

which only the strongest can survive. Riding on cobbles is hard enough – it is atrociously difficult even for the strongest professional cyclists. In 1994 persistent rain added to this difficulty, turning the roads into quagmires, covering the riders in thick mud and causing crash after crash. The formidable Russian Andrei Tchmil emerged from the chaos to take victory, riding away from the other favourites with 50km (31 miles) still to ride.

Liège–Bastogne–Liège

The oldest of the Classics is a hilly race in the Ardennes region of Belgium. It tends to attract the type of rider who is also a contender for the Tour de France – the constant climbing whittles down the field until only the strongest climbers are left.

Above: Hinault, this time battling through arctic conditions at the 1980 Liège–Bastogne–Liège.

Frenchman Bernard Hinault won the 1980 Liège–Bastogne–Liège in a terrible blizzard that besieged the riders throughout the race and subsequently wiped out more than half of the field. As rider after rider abandoned the race, Hinault forged ahead on his own, finishing 9 minutes ahead of the next rider. The cold was so terrible that Hinault never regained the feeling in one of his fingers.

Tour of Lombardy

The 'race of the falling leaves' takes place in northern Italy at the end of the cycling season. The race winds through the scenic wooded hills surrounding Lake Como – the biggest climb, the Madonna del Ghisallo, is named after the chapel at the top. Cycling fans consider this to be the most beautiful race of the season.

A race as hard as the Tour of Lombardy is usually won by solo escapers, but in 1983, a group of 13 riders poured into the finishing straight, including recently crowned world champion Greg

Above: Bernard Hinault en route to winning the 1980 World Championships in dominant style.

Lemond, and Irishman Sean Kelly, who would become one of the most prolific Classics winners of them all.

As the group sprinted towards the line, there was a blanket finish, with four riders flashing across the line. In first place was Kelly, only half a wheel ahead of Lemond.

The World Championships

Held at a different venue every year, the World Championships take place over a course based on laps of the same circuit. Unusually, riders compete for their country, rather than the professional trade teams they represent the rest of the year. The winner of the race is presented with a white jersey with rainbow stripes, which he has the right to wear in races for the next year.

In 1980 the course was more mountainous than it had ever been before, based at Sallanches in the French Alps. This coincided with French cyclist Bernard Hinault, a notoriously prickly character, coming back from injury, during which he had been written off by the media. He took his revenge by thrashing his rivals, attacking on the climb on each lap until he was on his own.

OFF-ROAD RACING

The next step up from riding off-road trails is racing
along them. With the boom in mountain biking,
off-road racing has grown along with the popularity of
the bikes themselves. Mountain bike cross-country racing
is now an Olympic sport, while thousands of people
enter long-distance enduro races.
The sport of cyclo-cross, which developed along with
the sport of road racing, has enjoyed a mini-boom
on the back of mountain biking. As people discover the
fun of racing mountain bikes, cyclo-cross gives them a
different opportunity to race off-road.

Above: Cross-country racing on mountain bikes has become more and more popular.
Left: Off-road racing is a tough but rewarding sport.

The Cross-country Race Bike

A good cross-country bike has to meet many requirements. Cross-country racing is technically demanding, testing physical strength and stamina and bike-handling ability across a wide variety of terrains.

In a cross-country race held on a small or medium-sized circuit, a rider can expect to encounter steep uphills, technical sections demanding occasional dismounting, twisty descents and long flat sections. Added to all that, the prevailing weather must also be taken into consideration. If it is raining, wet surfaces can completely change the character of a circuit. What is perfectly acceptable to ride on in the dry might be a totally different proposition in poor weather or in muddy conditions.

There is a perfect cross-country bike for each course, but most people cannot keep a stable of mountain bikes, all set up differently, to take down when they are needed. Sometimes, a compromise is necessary, in which case you should simply get a bike that you feel comfortable with and that suits you and your riding style.

Most cross-country courses include punishing technical sections that make great demands on both bike and rider, so it is also a good idea to emphasize reliability.

Anatomy of a cross-country race bike

❶ Suspension fork: Medium or short travel or 'give' – some shock absorbency is needed.

❷ Full-suspension frame: Greater shock absorbency is needed for technical sections of the races. Some models can lock out the suspension system for better conditions and easier terrain.

❸ Brakes: V-brakes are the lightest, most efficient option, and they provide good stopping power.

❹ Wheels: 26in spoked wheels.

❺ Tyres: Knobbly tyres are good for maximum traction. If the course has less in the way of loose surface, such as stones, semi-slicks can be substituted instead.

❻ Gears: Nine-speed freewheel. Gear levers are integrated with brake levers.

❼ Chainset: Triple chainset for a wide range of gears – some technical and steep sections need very low gears to prevent stalling.

❽ Pedals: Clipless pedals to be used with off-road shoes. Shoeplates can clip into either side of the pedal.

Choosing a cross-country bike

The first question is whether to go for hardtail or full suspension. The hardtail will be lighter uphill, but is much less comfortable and manoeuvrable down the other side. Until full-suspension bikes are made lighter, this choice will have to be made. With suspension, both at the forks and rear of the bike, travel is an important factor. For leisure riding, greater travel in the suspension gives a more comfortable ride. But racing riders want speed rather than comfort. Ideally there will be minimal travel in the forks and just enough travel in the rear to take the shock out of bumpy downhills.

Left: Suspension forks are needed for all but the easiest of cross-country courses, dampening the shock of hitting bumps, rocks and tree roots.

Top left: Many cross-country courses have technical sections that test riders' abilities to the limit.
Top: Powerful disc brakes help control speed.
Above: Thick, knobbly tyres are necessary for grip and traction.

Sizing is important. Cross-country racing bikes have a long top tube for aerodynamics and efficiency on long hills but a shorter bike is easier to pedal up short steep hills. Cross-country bikes use 26in wheels, with a width of between 1½ and 2in. The narrower the wheel, the lighter, but a 1½in wheel will be a compromise between lightness and durability. Tyre pressures need to be higher, so rough terrain is hard to ride on. On a fast, dry course, less tread gives a more efficient ride.

Cross-country Race Skills

Cross-country races can be won on your ability to go up and down hills successfully. Practice can really pay off in this situation. If you cannot climb, you will find it difficult to win a cross-country race because most courses are hilly.

By training for climbs and riding them effectively, your chances of victory or a top-ten finish will be increased. Even if you are well behind the leaders, riding to your own potential is a satisfying experience. While most hills will probably be short, steep sprints, there will still be significant amounts of climbing in most courses.

As well as training, there are two things you can do to lighten the load and increase your climbing speed – losing weight yourself, and losing weight from your bike. At the same time, work on your climbing technique and you will see big improvements.

The longer top tube typical on racing cross-country bikes is an aid to climbing – it stretches your upper body out and gives you a lower centre of gravity. Bar-end attachments will get you even lower.

Depending on the steepness and the surface, move backward and forward on the bike to maintain traction. A steep

climb needs more weight forward, while you can stay back for a steady climb. It may sometimes be necessary to climb out of the saddle but this reduces traction in the back wheel, so you must judge whether the terrain is suitable. Climbing out of the saddle can be useful when a hill is very steep or if you are trying to get to the top ahead of another competitor before reaching a technical section you want to lead.

Descending and cornering

While cross-country races can be won on the uphill sections, they can equally be won or lost in the downhills. Descending fast is an essential part of cross-country racing – you will need to be able to relax and stay controlled.

If you have a full-suspension bike, your job is already easier – by taking some of the shock out of the bumps,

Left: On less technical descents, keep your weight back and stay in control of your bike.

Above: Be careful of letting gaps go during uphill sections, and always be on the lookout for overtaking chances.

the suspension will allow you to control your line and bike much better.

To ride down steep hills fast, you need to allow the bike to do some of the work while you stay supple and relaxed. Get your weight back – on some very steep hills, you need to be well over the back wheel, with your stomach touching the saddle. Check your speed by feathering the back brake, and pick your line well ahead.

In corners, depending on your speed, the angle of the track and how sharp the bend itself is, the correct technique is to use shifts in your weight, as well as steering, to get round. With more body weight over the front wheel, you can gain traction and control.

Many bends are banked, which helps in getting round them – moderate your speed before you hit the bend, lean the bike over, keep your head at 90 degrees

Above: During complicated sections, keep your fingers over the brakes in case of sudden obstacles.
Left: Tackle descents that have obstacles with care. Stay relaxed and balanced.

to the ground, steer as much as you need to and let the banking and centrifugal force do the rest.

Planning and fuelling

For longer races, it is not enough to simply turn up and ride. Since no external assistance is allowed in cross-country racing, you have to help yourself in the case of mechanical trouble. You are also responsible for making sure that you eat and drink enough to prevent yourself running out of energy.

It is your choice how much mechanical gear you take with you in a race, but if finishing is a priority, then you will need to carry spare tubes, tyre levers and a chain breaker. With these tools you can improvise a repair that will get you up and running again.

For race food, modern energy bars and gels are light and take up very little space – in a long race you need to eat at least one energy bar or gel an hour.

They can be carried tucked into a pocket. Drink plenty of fluid, depending on the weather: experience will tell you how much you need.

Above: Aim to control your line and your bike when riding down a bumpy or rocky descent.
Above left: In longer races, riders have to refuel on the go. It's a good idea to keep an energy gel tucked in the shorts for easy access.

Cross-country Race Strategies

The difficult terrain of cross-country events is such that technique and tactics throughout the race really count if you are to win. As with most cycle races, trying to have a plan for every eventuality is the best bet.

At the start of a cross-country race it is crucial to get to the front as soon as possible. Courses tend to narrow down to a singletrack fairly quickly, making overtaking very difficult. The more people get in front of you at the start, the harder it is to make any headway on the leaders. Some starts are organized by race number or seeding, with the best riders on the front row, and the others in lines behind them. Others are based on order of arrival.

There are two things that will affect your initial placing in a race – your grid position, and yourself. If you are on the front line, you will have a clear run at the first corner. If you are back on the third row, you'll be fighting for position.

A good start, in either position, will significantly help your chances. Before the start, warm up thoroughly – your legs have to be ready for an immediate big effort. A physical warm-up is not the only necessity – go through the first minutes of the race mentally, which will get you focused on what you need to do.

When the starting gun goes, get clipped in quickly and go as hard as you can to get to or stay at the front. The sprint for the first corner, or the first narrow section, is as important as the sprint for the finish line. You need to be strong and determined, and able to recover quickly from the effort.

Pacing

Cross-country races, even short ones, are extremely hard work. Uphill sections build up lactic acid in the muscles. The start puts you into oxygen debt. Long technical sections of singletrack force you to constantly brake and accelerate. Even supporting your body weight and absorbing the shocks on the downhill sections is very hard. Fitness is crucial, and so is the ability to pace yourself. Trying too hard in the first half of a race can leave you with no energy in the second

Above: Cross-country mountain bike races start with all the riders in a group.

Above: Cross-country races involve consistent and intense efforts.

half but sitting back to save yourself for the second half will leave you well down the field, with stragglers blocking up the singletrack. Experience will tell you how hard you can go. But cross-country is not a time trial – it is a race against other people. Sometimes it is important to go harder or ease up. If you are a handful of seconds ahead of the rider behind and you know that there is a stretch of singletrack coming up, try to get there first. It's worth making the effort to stay ahead – they will find it difficult to get past once the singletrack starts, and you can recuperate there. If you are in second place, you know that a really hard dig for a few minutes will be worth it if you can get past.

Overtaking

Singletrack is great for technically skilful riders. During a singletrack section of a cross-country race, good bike handlers and trail riders come into their own.

On a singletrack, having the skills needed to overtake when you get stuck behind a slower rider is crucial. You could always wait until the next climb or wider track to overtake, but that might be several minutes away. Instead, you should press for a chance to overtake.

To overtake on singletrack takes acceleration and foresight. Follow your opponent's wheel, assuming he or she is on the racing line, and look past them for small gaps, or wider sections. Keep pressing, staying as close as possible,

Top left: Don't lose concentration during downhill sections.
Top middle: Always keep your eyes open for overtaking opportunities.
Top right: When you start to get tired, try to keep going and pace yourself.
Above left: The start of a race is a crucial time for getting into the best position.
Above: With luck, fitness and ability, comes victory.

so that when the opportunity presents itself you will be ready for it. When it comes, attack hard and try to surprise your opponent. If you can get your front wheel in front of theirs, you can dictate the racing line. The openings will be brief, but they are there to be taken.

Great Mountain Bike Races

The World Cup, the World Championships and the Olympics are big events for mountain bike competitors. Attracting the elite of international mountain bike riders, they are popular with tourists and also with aspiring riders.

In a notable series of mountain bike events that are scheduled around the world during the course of a year, four stand out.

The World Cup

In this event, riders win points in each round, which count towards an overall title at the end of the year in a variety of disciplines including cross-country, downhill and four-cross racing.

Events attract huge crowds, and the World Cup has evolved into the most important mountain biking competition in the world, after the Olympic Games. The various events have proved popular as tourist races – amateurs can ride on the same terrain and courses as their professional heroes.

Right: Ned Overend, a formidable and successful competitor in many mountain biking events.

Above: The Dane, Henrik Djernis, has won countless races in his long career.

The World Championships

The mountain bike World Championships started in 1990 and are now a one-off event held annually in a different venue every year. Disciplines added from 1992 include cross-country, trials riding, downhill and four-cross. The blue riband event is the men's cross-country race, which was first run in 1990 and won by US mountain biking legend Ned Overend. Winners of the events receive a gold medal and are eligible to wear the rainbow jersey for similar events for a year.

The World Championships are arranged by nationality rather than by teams, and are usually held at the end of the mountain biking season.

The most successful rider at the World event has been Danishman Henrik Djernis, who won three world championships in 1992, 1993 and 1994. In recent years Julien Absalon also won a hat trick, between 2004 and 2006.

Above: French mountain biker Julien Absalon won the Olympics in 2004.

The Olympic Games

The cross-country race has been part of the Olympic Games since 1996, and is seen as the pinnacle of mountain biking competition. It is the only form of mountain biking discipline practised at the Summer Olympics, and the gold medal winners have gone down in history as legends of the sport.

The first Olympic cross-country race for men in Atlanta 1996 was won by Dutchman Bart Brentjens, while Italian Paola Pezzo took the women's race. The Americans hosted the event with expectations of victory, but the home of mountain biking came away with nothing except a bronze medal in the women's race. Their top finisher in the men's race was Tinker Juarez in 19th place. France has performed well since then, having taken two gold medals in the men's cross-country race. Miguel Martinez dominated the Sydney Olympic race in 2000, while Julien Absalon was the winner in Athens in 2004.

The Sea Otter Classic

One of the biggest off-road cycling festivals in the world is the Sea Otter Classic. The World Championships, the World Cup and Olympic Games have the official stamp of approval, while the Sea Otter Classic welcomes amateur racers as well as the top elites. Sea Otter takes place in Monterey, California, and hosts events such as dirt-jumping, slalom, cross-country, downhill and elite-level races as well as trials demonstrations. The Classic attracts more than 50,000 mountain biking enthusiasts, and spectators and riders alike enjoy one of the largest cycling events of the year.

Above: Miguel Martinez on his way to a gold medal in the 2000 Summer Olympics in Sydney.
Below: Bart Brentjens, who won bronze in the 2004 Summer Olympics.

Left: The popular Sea Otter Classic in Monterey celebrates the sport of mountain biking with several events for all levels and all ages.

Cyclo-cross

The winter sport of cyclo-cross is the original off-road racing – it was around for years before mountain bikes came on to the scene. Cyclo-cross is very different from mountain biking; both take place off-road, but there the similarity ends.

A cyclo-cross bike looks more like a road bike than a mountain bike, with dropped handlebars and minimal extras. In a race, riders get off their bikes during steep sections and run with their bikes on their shoulders, sometimes for significant distances. Unlike mountain bike races, which are predicated on self-sufficiency, cyclo-cross races allow mechanical assistance. Riders often use two bikes in a race – one to ride, while the other is cleaned and prepared by a helper.

Obstacles along the way

Cyclo-cross races are short and sharp. They take place on a circuit, upon which the riders do enough laps for the race to last an hour. Like a mountain bike race, overtaking is difficult, with many circuits offering enough room for only one rider to pass. Circuits can incorporate muddy sections, wooded paths, sand, steep hills, cambered sections and occasionally even stretches of road. Tree roots and rocks have to be cycled over, jumped or riders simply have to dismount. Many organizers incorporate short sections of boarded jumps, about 30cm (12in) high, which have to be crossed on foot, although the 1989 world championships were won by Belgian Danny De Bie, who developed a technique of bunny-hopping the obstacles and staying on his bike while others wasted time dismounting, running and remounting. Depending on the time of year and weather, there may be obstacles such as water and ice. Coping with these challenges will improve your chances in a race.

Right: Weary cyclists carry their bikes during the Three Peaks cyclo-cross event in Yorkshire, England, which is one of the longest and toughest events in the world. It covers 61km (38 miles) over three of the highest hills in the country.

Mud

Cyclo-cross is referred to as 'mud-plugging', which describes the conditions encountered in a cyclo-cross race. After rain, the course becomes stickier and more slippery. Sticky mud gets into the tyre treads and the workings of your bike, adding to its weight and detracting significantly from its performance. A bike change every lap can help, but the mud soon builds up again, sapping your strength. Slippery mud comes with more rain. Keeping your balance is difficult, especially on cambered surfaces or around corners.

The main technique to use when riding in mud is to put the bike into a lower gear, and sit more upright, putting more weight on the pedals so that you are still sitting on the saddle but also letting your legs take the strain. This will give more traction. This takes a little weight off the handlebars, which results in a more relaxed riding style, and it leads on to another technique that is easier to do than explain. It involves letting the bike take some decisions for you – don't force it to follow a certain line. In really atrocious conditions, let some pressure out of your tyres to give more traction in the mud.

Dry conditions

You can approach a dry cyclo-cross course very differently from a muddy one, and the going will be easier and faster. Depending on the surface of the course, it might be worth putting on tyres with less tread and inflating them to a higher pressure. You will not need to change bikes so often, or perhaps at all – plan for this, and your race strategy will be more effective.

Roots and bunny hops

To ride over roots, lift your front wheel over them and let your back wheel follow. This way you can maintain maximum traction and acceleration.

To clear bunny hops, lift the front wheel first, pulling your arms up. Then, immediately pull up and backwards with your legs to get the back wheel over the obstacle. If they are too high, the only way is to jump off and run over them.

Ice and snow

The hardest surface of all to deal with is ice – the slightest deviation in your line, or on the surface, can have you off your

Left: Riders have to get off and run when bunny hops are too high to jump.

Above left: On muddy ground, riding becomes less efficient – sometimes it is faster to get off and run.
Above: When the weather is dry, races are much faster.
Below: Cyclo-crossers should be prepared for all kinds of conditions.

bike very quickly. Being able to avoid crashing on an icy course is a big advantage. The technique for riding on ice is to turn a big gear and sit low, to keep your centre of gravity nearer the ground. Fatter tyres, at a lower pressure, help to maintain grip.

Snow can be similar to mud and clogs up the workings of the bike, especially the brakes and the sprockets. For this you will need tyres with a deeper tread on the rear wheel and a file tread on the front.

The Cyclo-cross Bike

Cyclo-cross is a winter sport, so bikes are subject to constant abuse from rain, mud, sand and grit. Mud and dirt builds up in the crannies of the frame, in the brakes and in the gears, so to get a good performance from your bike, maintenance is essential.

Cyclo-cross bikes may look like road racing bikes, but they have a number of modifications that make them ideal for off-road racing. Bikes for cyclo-cross need to be as light as possible so that they are easier to carry. On a technical course, with steep hills, the riders will spend a great deal of time running with their bikes on their shoulders, and every extra gram counts. Comfort is a consideration, although most cyclo-cross events tend to be short at around an hour, so it is not as important as it would be with a mountain bike or a sportive bike.

Choosing a cyclo-cross bike

Cyclo-cross frames tend to be about 1cm (½in) shorter along the top tube than an equivalent road bike for the same rider. Aerodynamics are not as important, so riders sit more upright, with higher handlebars, and brake levers positioned higher up, giving a shorter position. Frame geometry differs – a shallower seat angle, and a moved-back saddle pushes the rider back so that their weight is farther over the rear wheel. This helps steering and control and adds traction over rough terrain.

Anatomy of a cyclo-cross bike

❶ Frame: Lightweight for easier carrying, with large clearances to avoid mud build-up.

❷ Wheels: Lightweight, for easier carrying. Mud builds up on spokes, so modern wheels have fewer of them. V-shaped rims are easier to clean. Size is usually 700x28C, but larger or smaller wheels can be used according to conditions.

❸ Tyres: Fat and knobbly for extra traction on loose surfaces. Pressures are lower than for road tyres, which also helps traction.

❹ Chainset: Single, double or triple chainrings, according to terrain. A triple offers more gears, but weighs more. Generally, double is most popular, using 39–48. Cranks are marginally longer than a typical road bike.

❺ Sprockets: Nine-speed freewheel with 13–26 sprockets.

❻ Brakes: Cantilever brakes avoid mud build-up. Brake levers incorporate gear levers for accessibility. Some riders ride with an extra pair of brakes on the top, with separate cables to the brakes.

❼ Handlebars: High handlebars for an upright position, with dropped ends, for use when accelerating.

❽ Pedals: Clipless pedals to be combined with an off-road shoe.

Above: Cyclo-cross bikes have to be set up to deal with clogging mud.
Right: Riders in cyclo-cross events need to be prepared to spend a lot of time running with their bike.

The clearances on a cyclo-cross frame are large, with no bridge between the chainstays, and the fittings are designed to take cantilever brakes. These have separate calliper arms attached to pivot points on the frame and forks, joined by a central cable that runs to the brake levers. The advantage of cantilever brakes is that they do not clog up with mud.

Wheels need to be lightweight. Carbon composite wheels can be used, which have fewer spokes and are very easy to clean. On these wheels, the braking surface is aluminium, for better performance. Carbon wheels are an expensive option, however, and a set of lightweight spoked wheels will also offer good performance. Deep, V-shaped rims are less likely to clog up around the spokes, and are easier to clean.

Tyres need good traction. Cyclo-cross tyres are knobbly to prevent slipping.

It is possible to ride cyclo-cross races with single, double or triple chainrings, according to the terrain. A single chainring saves weight, but there will be

Above left: Cyclo-cross bikes are similar to road bikes, but note the thicker tyres and cantilever brakes.
Above right: Stay upright when riding through challenging or technical sections.

fewer gears. Doubles are the best option generally, using a 39–48 combination, with 13–26 sprockets at the back. In very steep terrain, a triple might be necessary, but it is often easier to get off and run up steep hills because of the rough ground.

Cyclo-cross Skills

Racing cyclo-cross requires a wider set of skills than racing on the road. Accidents apart, road racers mount once and dismount once, before and after a race. Cyclo-crossers may do this 50 times or more in the course of a race so it's an important skill to perfect.

Running with the bike on your shoulder will be quicker than riding in many situations. You should learn to dismount and mount in relaxed, confident movements, making them part of the forward progress of your bike.

When and how to dismount

The reasons for dismounting are a steep hill, or an obstacle that you cannot jump the bike over or ride around. On a steep hill, first try riding out of the saddle with your weight back to maintain traction. If the hill is too steep, dismount from the bike. In the approach to the dismount, ride in an upright position, with your hands on the brake hoods. Unclip your right foot and swing it over the back of the saddle, and grab the top tube with your right hand as you jump off. Unclip the left foot. With the bike still moving, start running as your feet hit the ground, and lift your bike on to your shoulder. If the hill you are about to ride up is rideable at the bottom, don't

Dismounting from your bike

1: *Approach a dismount with your hands on the brake hoods.*

2: *Unclip your right foot and start to swing your leg over the saddle.*

Handling on slippery hills

Cyclo-cross climbs are short and steep, and the fastest way up when they are rideable is to ride out of the saddle with your hands on the brake hoods. But the muddier the ground, the harder it is to gain traction. When it is especially slippery, stay out of the saddle, but try to put your weight back over your rear wheel to prevent it from slipping, and ride in as straight a line as possible.

Descending is straightforward – hold the drops, and relax, with your weight set back to keep traction, and staying out of the saddle so you can use your legs as shock absorbers. If you feel the bike slipping, or you can see an especially difficult section coming up, unclip one foot from the pedal and touch it to the ground for balance.

3: *Unclip your left foot and jump from the bike.*

4: *Lift your bike on to the shoulder or, if you are tall, hold the frame.*

dismount until then. Try not to grind to a halt, but swing your right leg over, keeping both hands on the brake levers. Jump off, push the bike along the ground to maintain momentum, then pick the bike up. Running with a bike unbalances your natural rhythm and weighs you down. Carry the bike with the top tube on your right shoulder, with the wheel turned inward. Taller riders may find it more comfortable to hold the head tube with one arm, and the handlebars with the other. Shorter riders hook their arm under the down tube, and hold on to the drop of the handlebar. Most running sections are short, so concentrate on strong running.

How to remount

Once you have cleared the obstacle, remount. Grab the top tube with your right hand, and put the bike on the ground. Push forward to get moving again, at the same speed as you are running. Put both hands on the brake hoods and jump back into the saddle, with your right leg over the back wheel. Once you are on the saddle, look down to the pedals, and clip both feet in.

Climbing

Climbing: *When climbing, keep your weight back over the rear wheel.*

How to run with your bike

Running: *Lift the bike on to your shoulder, or if you are tall, hold it by the frame. Look ahead to where you are going and stay upright, relaxed and balanced.*

Remounting your bike

1: *Put your bike on the ground while you are still running.*

2: *Place your hands on both handlebars before remounting.*

3: *Jump back on, swinging your right leg over the saddle.*

4: *Land in the saddle as you clip in with your left foot.*

TRACK RACING

Track riding is bike racing at its purest. The bikes have a single gear, with a fixed wheel system that prevents freewheeling. They have no brakes – sudden braking is not necessary, and the legs can be used to slow the bikes down. Riders race around a velodrome – a steep, banked oval track, either indoor or outdoor. The banking helps keep the speed high by counteracting the centrifugal force that normally pulls riders out on bends. Track racing is fast and furious, with spectacular races and unique athletic challenges.

Above: In the Madison relay race, one rider propels another into 'play'.
Left: Specialized track races take place in a velodrome.

The Track Bike

Track bikes are the minimalist art of the bike world; they are pared-down lightweight models. The designs are highly specialized, and there are almost as many different types of track bikes as there are events.

Sprinters' bikes need to be as stiff as possible, to withstand the considerable force applied during acceleration. Pursuit riders add tri-bars to their bikes for more aerodynamic positions, and their frames need less steep angles than the sprinters.

It is impractical for most riders interested in riding track to own a different bike for each race, so most track bikes are capable of being used in all events, with small adjustments for each event if necessary.

Track bikes are built for speed and efficiency. While road bikes are often a compromise between the stiffness needed to ensure effective transmission of energy and comfort over long distances, there is no compromise with track bikes. The stiffer the better in this case, since you will not be doing any long rides on your track bike.

Specification of a track bike

Track frames have a shorter wheelbase, and positions are often set more aggressively than on road bikes, with lower handlebars for better aerodynamics. The biggest difference between track bikes and road bikes is in the gearing. Although component manufacturers have been adding more sprockets on to the back wheel of a road bike – from five in the 1970s to ten 30 years later – the track bike still has only one gear. Riders accelerate, cruise and sprint in the same gear, and a lockring on the rear gearing prevents freewheeling. Riders must choose a gear based on their experience and training.

The wheels are built for lightness and stiffness. Many riders favour a solid carbon fibre rear disc and spoked front wheel. The front wheels also may be

Above: Track bikes have a single chainring at the front and a single sprocket at the back, giving only one gear.
Below: Track bikes are pared down to the minimum, so that very high speeds can be reached.

carbon fibre, with deep rim sections and three or four spokes to reduce air resistance. Handlebars are deep and narrow. For racing, riders need only use the drops, so the tops of the bars are minimal. With bars set closer to the bike, riders can use their arms and upper body to pull up while pushing down on the pedals, to gain extra power.

Right: Track bikes don't have brakes – to decelerate, just slow down pedalling rate.

Anatomy of a track bike

❶ **Frame and forks:** Ultra-stiff carbon fibre one-piece frame. Frames are light, but low flexibility under acceleration is most important. Steep angles give a more responsive, albeit less comfortable ride.

❷ **Rear disc wheel:** Solid, and more stiff and aerodynamic than a spoked wheel. Attached to the frame with a fixed nut, rather than a quick release, to withstand the force of acceleration.

❸ **Front wheel:** Stiff, aerodynamic carbon fibre deep section rims with minimum number of spokes for less air resistance, or solid, as here.

❹ **Tyres:** Lightweight tubular tyres for less rolling resistance and weight.

❺ **Chainring:** Single lightweight chainring.

❻ **Sprocket:** Single sprocket gives only one gear ratio, so gear selection is crucial. Hub is fixed to prevent freewheeling.

❼ **Handlebars:** Deep handlebars, set in close to the bike for greater aerodynamics, and to give maximum pull during acceleration.

❽ **Saddle:** Comfortable and supportive.

❾ **Pedals:** Clipless road pedals. For some events, in which acceleration is important, riders also strap their feet to the pedals for extra security and power.

Track Racing Skills: Getting Started

Track riding is a bit more limited than road riding in the sense that if you don't live near a velodrome, it is difficult to practise, whereas on the road, you can just go out and train. If your ambitions lie on the track, find your nearest velodrome and arrange to train there.

If you can only ride on a velodrome twice a month, make the most of the sessions on the track, and work on your endurance, speed and power on a road bike. Many countries boast velodromes and the sport is very popular in Europe, particularly in France, Germany, Belgium and the United Kingdom. Japan and Australia have also taken up track racing, and it is included in the Summer Olympic Games and also the Track World Championships.

Starting out

Even if you are an experienced bike rider, it is worth taking time and care over the transition to a track bike and

Right: When riding in a bunch on the track, keep your head up in case of riders changing direction in front of you.

Above: Track riders must be comfortable riding in large groups.

Above: To attack, riders accelerate, then jump hard to quickly make a gap.

riding on a velodrome. When a rider wants to stop, the natural reflex, built up over years of cycling, is to stop pedalling and apply the brakes, but there are no

brakes, and it is impossible to freewheel on a track bike. The result of trying to do this can be undignified, at best, as the momentum of the pedals going

round throws the unsuspecting road rider off the bike. Stopping a track bike is an acquired skill. At the end of a race or ride, just slow down gradually, circling the track as you do so. As you come to a halt, lean up against the track wall or railings, so you can unclip safely. If you

Above: When riding around a bend in the velodrome, it is very important to maintain your balance.

need to stop more quickly, use your legs as brakes by fighting against the turn of the pedals. Keep your balance and make sure the upper body is providing a good anchor for your legs. After a while you will be able to control your speed with variations in pedalling technique.

Riding on a velodrome track for the first time can also be difficult. The banking on the corners, especially on smaller tracks, seems quite steep. It is important to ride positively into a corner, especially when you are inexperienced. The banking is there to guide you round

Above: Rebecca Romero and the UK team on their way to winning the Women's Team Pursuit in the Track World Championships of 2008.

the corner without losing speed, so concentrate on getting up to a good speed, then holding your line as you hit the bend. Do not be tempted to turn left (down), as you will come off the banking and lose speed. Instead, follow the bend round until the exit. It is an exhilarating experience, and the more you do it, the more your confidence will grow. If you follow the golden rule of holding your speed and line, your progress round the bend will be constant.

Gaining speed

Banking on a track not only keeps your bike in a straight line when you go around corners, it can also help you to accelerate in a race. If you ride in a straight line around the banking, you are essentially riding along the flat. By riding up the banking, to the top, you have ridden up a hill. Correspondingly, it is downhill from there to the bottom of the track. Sprinters often use this technique to gain extra acceleration. To do this, move to the outside of the

Right: To perform a track stand, turn the wheel up the track and balance carefully.

track before the corner, and follow the line round at the top of the bank. Once you are round the apex of the bend, accelerate hard, and turn inward so that you can take advantage of the downhill slope to boost your speed. You should not cross anyone's racing line while you are doing this, although professional track sprinters take their riding right up to the limit of this rule. One disadvantage is that by riding around the outside you are riding farther than your rival, but this is balanced by the extra acceleration. Experience will show you when to use this tactic.

Track Racing Skills: Group Riding

Most track events involve riding in a bunch. With limited space on the track, riders must co-operate, as well as compete with each other. When riding in a bunch, individuals must develop a keen sense of awareness, and anticipate what others are going to do.

Riding with other people is especially important in the keirin event, where six sprinters race against each other, and the team pursuit, where four team-mates have to work together to ride as fast as possible. In each case, you will be riding at great speed in close proximity to other riders, and your safety relies on everybody being capable of riding in a group situation.

Bunches of riders move efficiently around velodromes, if everyone rides in a straight line and holds that line around the bends. It gets complicated when, as often happens in a bike race, certain riders want to move past other riders.

Manoeuvres take place in a spirit of general co-operation, within certain boundaries. Riders are responsible for

Below: Riders must be aware of the situation of the whole bunch and look around to check where other cyclists are positioned.

Above: When the speed in a race increases, the group lines out into single file – riders must not let gaps go.

their own actions and for knowing what is happening around them. You should be constantly looking ahead and focusing on what is happening. You can hear riders behind you, and occasionally look behind with a small glance, just to make sure nobody is coming up fast. If you want to move up, once you are sure nobody is coming up fast behind you, give a small signal by flicking your elbow out on the side you want to move into. Then make your move. Communication is important. Riders shout to let each other know if they are coming up fast,

or if you move out too suddenly. Keep your movements flowing, rather than sudden – this maintains the speed and momentum of the bunch, avoids making enemies, and will allow for smoother, more efficient acceleration.

Sprinting

When sprinting, choose and hold your line, and respect that of other riders. In a scratch race, when sprinting for first place at the finishing line, 10 or 15

Above: One momentary lapse of concentration can cause a crash – take care to stay out of trouble.

riders, or even more, can be jockeying for position across the track. Never move across someone's line, and trust that they will not do the same to you. It's a good idea to get into a good position at the front before the final sprint starts, so you can avoid the jostling farther back. In a team pursuit, or during a breakaway,

Above: This shows the point in a race when riders are holding a straight line around bends.

Above: In a race, if you ride directly behind another rider, you will save yourself effort.

Golden rules of track riding

1 Keep pedalling
You should always keep your legs moving on your track bike – with no freewheel, you have no choice but to pedal while the bike is moving, and your legs control your speed. The constant pedalling can have a beneficial effect on your pedalling style for other forms of riding and on the suppleness of your legs.

2 Keep your line
You will obviously need to move from side to side occasionally in order to pass riders, but there is a definite etiquette to follow, based around the idea that no rider should put another rider in danger. When moving out, signal with a flick of your arm that you are going to do so.

3 Keep your head horizontal
When going around the bend, don't hold your head at 90 degrees to the sloping track; hold it horizontal to the ground. This will help you keep your balance and judge the steepness of the banking.

4 Be aware of those around you
Keep an eye on the riders ahead, and turn around every so often to check what is going on behind you. Know where the other riders are and what they are doing, and you can use this to your advantage.

5 Vary the pace
The greatest skills in track riding are being able to accelerate fast, and hold a high cruising speed. If you can do this in a race, your chances of success are much higher.

6 Concentrate
Things happen very quickly in track races, including crashes. Be ready to react to everything that happens in front of you.

riders work in groups as in a road race. The best way is to ride in a line, one behind the other, because there are no crosswinds to make group riding more efficient. Each rider does a turn, then swings up the banking, keeping the same speed, but adding distance so the others can move up on the inside. The first rider drops into last position in the line.

Track Racing: Scratch Race, Points Race and the Madison

Track racing has evolved an esoteric and unusual group of events, perhaps because tracks are so uniform across the world. To provide entertainment and variety for the crowds, different styles of racing have developed.

Track racing is basically divided into two types of event – endurance and short distance. The short-distance events are the explosive ones – sprinting, kilometre time trials, and an event that originated in Japan called the keirin.

Endurance events include the pursuits, individual and team, and races such as the points race, scratch race and the Madison.

Scratch race

The most straightforward on the track, the scratch race is a distance race that is held over a number of laps or of kilometres, and the first rider across the line is the winner. The bunch does not ride the distance and just wait for the sprint finish, however. Like riders in a road race who want to neutralize a sprinter by attacking early, track riders don't want to pull a fast sprinter all the way to the last corner and see them sweep to victory. The scratch race is often full of attacks, counterattacks, splits and politics.

When racing a scratch race, it is a good idea to do your research first. Find out who is riding, who is a good sprinter and who is better at long drawn-out efforts. Make sure the sprinter is not in a position to go for victory, and watch for meaningful attacks by the latter kind of rider. There is no need to follow every attack through the race, but when a good long-distance rider goes, try to get into their slipstream, and see what you can do to gain a gap by working with anybody else who has made the split.

The advantage of racing in a velodrome is that once you have a gap of 100m (330ft) or more, you can see your pursuers on the other

side of the track. Keep an eye on them. When they string out it means that they are going faster, so inject a little more effort into your breakaway work, sharing to maintain the gap. If your break proves to be successful, you'll be in the sprint for the win. If it does not, just sit back in the bunch and gather your resources before making your next attack.

Above: In a scratch race, the first rider across the line wins, and the race is full of attacks and counter-attacks.

Points race

The winner of the points race is not necessarily the rider who crosses the line first at the finish. Over the course of the points race, there is a sprint, usually every 10 laps, for which points are awarded to the first four riders over the line. Throughout the race, each rider accumulates more points, and the rider with the most points at the finish is declared the winner. Some sprints offer double points.

The best way of guaranteeing a win in the points race would be to win every sprint. Since this scenario is unlikely, tactics start to come into play.

The most basic tactic involves going for every sprint, so that you have at least some chance each time. This is highly energy-consuming, although it can be an effective way of racing. There is a risk of spreading yourself too thinly, however, and tiring yourself for the crucial sprints later in the race.

The other method is to sit back and not contest the first two or three sprints. Save yourself and keep your resources for a big effort at the last sprint before halfway. If you can win this, you have a good foundation for the second half of the event.

The riders who have spent energy going for the first sprints may be too tired to match you. However, you should be careful of letting anyone accumulate too big a lead. The points race demands that you think on your feet because you may have to change your tactics later.

The Madison

This is an unusual event that involves teams of two riders competing in a system similar to the points race. In the Madison points are awarded in certain sprints through the race, and the winning team is the one with the most points.

Where things differ from the points race is in the style of racing. One rider from each team is 'in play' at any one

Above: In the 2008 Olympics, Bradley Wiggins (right) and Mark Cavendish (left) won gold for Great Britain in the Madison event.

moment. Teams work in a relay, swapping over, with one rider in the race, and the other resting. While the rider 'in play' competes, the other rider circles the track at the top and waits for their partner to approach. Once the partner is within a certain distance they accelerate, drop down, and then, using a method known as a handsling, are catapulted into the race, becoming the rider 'in play'.

The Madison is often confusing to watch, because slower riders circling the track at the top can distract from the race, and while teams are swapping over, it can be difficult to follow where the bunch exactly is.

An effective Madison partnership usually involves a good sprinter and a good endurance rider. The sprinter can gain laps, by attacking and lapping the field. Then the endurance rider works hard at maintaining the lead.

Left: A Madison handsling almost completed – the higher rider of the pair will accelerate away with the momentum of the handsling.

Track Racing: Pursuits, Kilometre Time Trial, Sprint and Keirin

Different kinds of track racing demand very different tactics and skills. The pursuit events need pure endurance over a longer distance, while the kilometre time trial is a harder, shorter event. The sprint and keirin are tactical battles between riders.

Left: Bradley Wiggins of Great Britain speeds to victory and a gold medal in the individual pursuit race in the Beijing Olympics in 2008.

Unlike the races on the previous pages, the pursuit events, kilometre time trial, sprint and keirin don't involve large bunches of riders. The individual pursuit pits two individuals against each other, usually over a distance of 3 or 4km, while the team pursuit does the same with two teams of four riders, over 5km. The kilometre time trial is an individual race against the clock, while the sprint and keirin pit two and six riders respectively against each other in a dash to the line.

Individual pursuit

The individual pursuit is a 4km time-trial event in which two riders start on opposite sides of the track, and set off at the same time. They are racing both against each other and against the clock. The race is over when both riders complete the 4km. If one rider can manage to catch up with the other, the race is declared over.

In major championships, the competitors ride a timed heat over the distance, with the top eight going through to the knockout round, where they are seeded according to their result. The pursuit attracts thoroughbred endurance riders, and many pursuiters develop into very good road riders. The distance is long enough that pace judgement, gearing and pain tolerance are very important. Of all the events on the track, it is easiest to start too fast in the pursuit. This results in a gradual and painful deceleration over the course of the 4km. Ideally, the 1km splits in a pursuit should be more or less identical, save for a slower first lap which takes into account accelerating from a standing start.

Team pursuit

Racing in a team pursuit works on exactly the same lines as the individual pursuit, except that there are four riders involved in each team. Team pursuit riding is as physically demanding as the individual pursuit, and imposes extra mental demands on the riders. A well-co-ordinated team rides in a perfectly straight line, with only centimetres between their front and back wheels. Riders work together, sharing the work to overcome air resistance. To change leaders, the front rider swings up the track on a bend, allowing the others to overtake on the inside. The leader then swings immediately back down, joining the line flawlessly in last place. Any error in judgement here can result in the rider dropping too far back, and not being able to keep up with the team. Although the time of the team is taken on the third rider to cross the line, a three-person team cannot easily match a four-man team.

Even start order is important in the team pursuit. Your slowest starter should be last in line for the first lap – they will start at the top of the track, and the slight banking in the straight will give them a small downhill, making up for their slower acceleration.

Kilometre time trial

For this race, riders are timed individually over a distance of 1km – the fastest rider wins. While the concept is simple, 1km is an extremely difficult distance to judge pace at. It is farther than the body is capable of maintaining at a sprint, but is not far enough to settle into a rhythm. It is one of the most painful disciplines in cycling, because of this difficulty. Riders often start too fast, resulting in cramping during the last lap as lactic acid builds up in their muscles.

The best way to approach a kilometre is to start fast, hold speed through to the last quarter, then do everything you can to hold on as the pain really kicks in.

Sprint

The sprint is a head-to-head event between two riders over a kilometre, although only the last 200m is timed. The riders circle the track, watching each other closely, before one of them launches their sprint, which can happen at any time, but tends to be in the latter stages of the race. The first across the line is the winner.

Sprinting gains its tactical subtleties from the fact that it is usually easier to win a sprint from behind another rider, thanks to the shelter from air resistance.

Below: Competing in the tough team pursuit event at the 2008 Olympics in Beijing resulted in a gold medal for the cycling team from Great Britain.

Riders will do everything they can to avoid having to lead out. As they slowly circle the track, the rider in the lead might try and force the other into the lead by jumping suddenly. In order to prevent being left behind, the opponent will react. The original leader slows down dramatically, while the opponent goes past him, taking the lead. Some sprinters start the sprint from a long way out, hoping that their rival does not have the endurance to be able to hold their speed to the end. Others prefer to wait, using devastating acceleration over a short distance to win.

Keirin

This is a race for a pure sprinter. The keirin originated in Japan. It is a sprint event in which a line of six riders is brought up to speed using a pacing rider, or more commonly a motorized bike called a 'derny'. Riders jockey for position following the derny – as the derny is providing shelter, there is no disadvantage to leading. With a certain distance to go, the derny peels off, and the riders are left to fight out the sprint.

Above: Chris Hoy of Great Britain wins the battle of the sprint, and the gold medal, at the 2008 Olympics in Beijing.

Track Racing: The Hour Record and Six-day Racing

The hour record is the blue riband of track racing. It is one of the hardest experiences riders can put themselves through on a bike, requiring immense skill, stamina and strength, as well as willpower, yet it is also one of the simplest.

Two events that rate as the most popular on the track are the hour record and six-day racing. The hour record is extremely arduous, while the six-day racing is very entertaining.

The hour record

Riding the maximum possible distance in an hour, around a velodrome, is called the 'hour record'. It demands constant, all-out exertion for the entire hour, with no chance to rest or freewheel. Because of its difficulty, very few riders attempt it, and winners gain great prestige. Sometimes the hour record is ridden at high altitudes, which confers an aerodynamic benefit on the rider because of the thin air. The design of the bike affects performance and innovative aerodynamic equipment has

Below: Olympic gold medallist Chris Boardman setting the 'athlete's' hour record at Manchester velodrome in 2000.

Above: Graeme Obree in the contentious 'superman' position, which he invented for the arduous hour record, one of the most physically difficult events in cycling.

been specially built. The hour record has belonged to some of the finest riders in the history of the sport – Fausto Coppi, Jacques Anquetil, Eddy Merckx and Miguel Indurain have all held it. These riders won 17 Tours de France between them. Merckx described the hour record he set in 1972 as the hardest event he had ever ridden.

The hour record entered the modern era in 1984 when Francesco Moser beat Eddy Merckx's long-standing record. While Merckx rode on a normal bike, with normal wheels and handlebars, Moser used a low-profile time-trialling machine with disc wheels. British rider Graeme Obree broke Moser's record in 1993, using a radical new position on the bike, known as the 'tuck'. Obree famously constructed his own bike for the record, with bottom bracket bearings taken from the drum of a washing machine. His compatriot Chris Boardman broke the record next, followed by Indurain and Swiss rider Tony Rominger. When Obree's position was banned by the cycling authorities, he developed yet another new position, the 'superman'. Boardman used the position and rode an astonishing 56.375km (35 miles). Although the 'superman' was controversial, the authorities granted Boardman the record, but banned the position.

There is now an 'athlete's' hour record, for which riders have to ride bikes similar to Merckx's when he broke the record.

Below: Track racing attracts many spectators at events across Europe.

Right: The Madison is one of the staples of six-day racing, drawing large crowds and elite riders.

Six-day racing

A six-day is an unusual type of cycling event held at velodromes in the winter that is part bike race and part circus. Originally, a six-day was just six solid days of racing, including at night. Since this much exertion is unreasonable, even by the tiring standards of bike racing, it has evolved into a race meeting where riders compete every evening for six days, in a variety of events.

Crowds at six-day races are huge. The Ghent six-day event, which takes place in Belgium every November, is one of the most atmospheric experiences in cycling. The velodrome at Ghent is tiny – the track is only 166m (545ft), with steep banking, and crowds are allowed into the centre of the track as well as in the stands. The riders speed past, within inches of the audience. Events include sprints and points races, but the real draw for the crowds is the nightly Madison event, which attracts the biggest names. There is a Madison classification similar to that in a stage race, where accumulated laps and points are added to a total to find the overall winner of the six-day racing.

ADVANCED TRAINING

In order to improve top-end fitness, racing cyclists need to incorporate high-intensity workouts into their training regime. By using interval training, riders can achieve a specific kind of fitness that will enable them to compete at the front of races. It is important to look after the body, by rest and recuperation, and by refuelling and nutrition strategies. You should also know how to deal with injury, if it occurs.

Above: Serious racing requires serious training on a regular basis.
Left: A racing cyclist is all kitted out to do some high-intensity riding.

Advanced Endurance Training and Specialized Drills

Base-building is one of the most important parts of training for cycling. By building endurance through regular, long steady distance rides, you prepare your body for the more intensive training that is to come later on.

Even when you are concentrating on speed work, it is important not to forget to work on your endurance. If you have spent several months building it up, it would be a shame to let it slip back.

If you are not racing over a weekend, try instead to go for a varied long ride, with sprints, long periods of hard efforts and hard climbing. The difference between this and a fartlek ride (alternating strenuous and normal effort) is that you rest more during the latter.

Long, varied endurance ride

You can do this type of ride with a group or on your own. Go out for a ride that is as long as your longest LSD (long steady distance) ride, but really vary the pace. Once you have warmed up, do some long climbs, and then try some extended periods when you are cruising at a good tempo. Include a couple of sprints. Keep up a high level of effort throughout.

For this advanced endurance ride, keep your effort steady between the harder efforts. Depending on the length of race you are training for, this sportive or enduro ride might be as long as 4 or 5 hours.

When building distance up over a period of weeks, a gradual increase is far preferable to a sudden increase. It is a

Below: On a long training ride, build endurance by keeping a steady effort over varied terrain, including long climbs.

good idea to incorporate an increase into your weekly distance, or the distance of your longest ride, then follow that by a week with no increase. By plateauing in this way, your body will compensate and be ready for the next increase.

The reason it is important to maintain and increase your endurance is that it improves your body's ability to use the glycogen stored in your muscles and liver. Your body will become more efficient at using glycogen as fuel, while at the same time burning larger amounts of fat. Your muscles will also become efficient at producing the movements necessary for cycling. As endurance is maintained and increased, your capacity for more specialized training is maintained and increased.

Specialized drills

Regular endurance training and interval training are very good for boosting your body's physiological abilities. You also need to pay attention to the skills you use in a road race, especially sprinting and climbing. The physical effort is very important, but you also have to hone your technique, so that you are sprinting and climbing with as much economy as possible.

Sprint training

During a long ride, include some sprint drills as you normally would, but focus on technique as well as physical effort. Keep your bike in a straight line, and maintain a strong upper body and core, using the arms to pull up on the bars while your legs work at turning the pedals round. Especially work on your initial jump, by seeing how quickly you can accelerate to maximum speed.

Climbing training

On the hills, follow the correct line round all the corners, focusing on sitting upright and relaxing the body, while spinning a low gear at 90–100 revolutions per minute or more. Hold the bars firmly, without gripping tightly. Practise varying the pace, even if you are not a natural climber. Attack hard out of the saddle, sit back down again to recover, accelerate slightly, then ride steadily to the top before sprinting the final 50m (164ft).

Above: During sprint training, build a series of maximum effort sprints into a medium-distance ride.
Below: Training with a group for long rides can be beneficial in alleviating boredom.

Interval Training

The training schedules in the following pages of this book are designed for sportive, enduro and fitness-oriented individuals, and will build a good base for this kind of cycling. Interval training alternates high-speed intense training and rest or low activity.

The intensity of a short race is much higher than that in a sportive or enduro event. The reason many people get dropped in a road or mountain bike race is not because they are not fit enough to ride the distance, but because they are not fit enough to ride at the same speed as their rivals. The frustrating thing is that often, the intense periods in a race don't last that long, but by that time, inexperienced or less fit riders are off the back. Race training therefore has to aim to cope with these larger stresses on the body. To do this you have to imitate the efforts made in a race situation, and the best way to do this is through interval training.

Interval training basically involves riding hard for a set period of time, usually between 1 minute and 10 minutes or so, then resting for a set recovery period, then repeating three or more times. Confusingly, the 'on' phase of the workout is known as the 'interval'.

Most intervals are precisely set at or slightly above your body's lactate threshold (see box). They are very effective at increasing fitness, but you do need to have a solid base of steady miles in your legs before you attempt them. The greater your endurance, built up over time, the higher the level of fitness you can achieve through intensive training. You should always be flexible about interval training – if you are tired before you even start, doing a full set might be counterproductive. Go for a recovery ride instead, and postpone your intervals for a couple of days.

The improvement in fitness levels from interval training means that from one week to the next, you'll need to increase the length of your intervals, or the frequency. If you are going to embark on a programme of interval training, it is essential to buy a pulse monitor, which will help you measure your effort correctly. Going too hard or

Above: Sportive events can be gruelling so it is important to be fit to begin with.

too easily will defeat the purpose of the training. Don't overdo it. It's important to keep increasing the length or intensity of your intervals according to your schedule, to get fitter.

Classic intervals

These are the most straightforward intervals you can do, and are an ideal way of introducing your body to the stress of the harder training. Make sure that you have been doing tempo rides for several weeks before you start doing these intervals. Once you are ready for interval training, the most important thing to do on these sessions is warm up properly. Spin your legs at a level of effort between easy and moderate for 20 or 30 minutes. When your warm-up is complete, find a flat bit of road with no junctions or traffic lights. Increase your effort to your lactate threshold for 6 minutes. Concentrate on smooth pedalling style, relaxing your upper body, and maintaining a steady pace.

Lactate threshold

During exercise, your muscles release lactic acid, a by-product of the process by which carbohydrates are converted into energy. When glycogen, stored in the muscles and liver, is metabolized, it is converted into energy, in the form of a molecule called adenosine triphosphate (ATP). The waste product from this process is lactic acid.

Lactic acid is what causes the burning sensation and pain in your muscles when you are exercising hard. At moderate or low levels of exercise, the body is capable of getting rid of lactic acid as fast as it builds up – this means that the body can maintain the same level of exertion. This is known as aerobic exercise; it uses a combination of fat and carbohydrates for fuel, and oxygen is used in converting this fuel to energy. The higher the intensity of exercise, the more carbohydrates are used as fuel, and the more

lactic acid builds up. But at more intense levels of exertion, the metabolism converting your muscles' fuel into energy goes from aerobic to anaerobic – oxygen delivery can no longer keep up with the demand. Beyond this point, your ability to sustain the effort is limited – if you sprint up a hill, you will probably experience an oxygen deficit. Anaerobic exercise relies on burning carbohydrates for fuel. When the body switches to anaerobic energy production, lactic acid builds up faster than your system can get rid of it. The point at which this happens is known as the lactate threshold, and it happens at a certain percentage of your maximum heart rate, depending on the individual. Scientific testing to measure blood lactate levels can find what your lactate threshold is, and will enable you to train effectively, with workouts based on exertions that are at, or just beyond, your threshold.

Suggested workouts

Some of the hill workouts can be adapted for interval training – doing your interval workouts on climbs can be a very effective way of ensuring that you are working hard enough. Don't work too hard – intervals are not sprints or speed work – the point is to train your body to maintain intense efforts over long periods. Remember that even the best sprinters in the world can't sprint all out for longer than 15 or 20 seconds.

Right: Training at high intensity gets your body used to the suffering it will encounter in a race.

Don't just push down on the pedals, but use these training sessions to work on pulling the pedals up and building a smooth pedal revolution.

After your 6-minute interval is up, recover for 3 minutes by riding at a similar pace to your warm-up. The pace should be moderate, but not slow. Then repeat the sequence three more times for a total of four intervals.

When you have done this workout twice, change the length of the interval to 7 minutes, but keep the rest period at 3 minutes. Keep adding a minute every two sessions until you can sustain the pace for four sets of 10-minute intervals.

High-intensity intervals

After a few weeks of regular classic intervals, you will be ready for some intervals of a higher intensity. For these workouts, always warm up well. Ride for 3 minutes just above your lactate threshold, and rest for 3 minutes before repeating three more times for a total of four intervals. Increase the length of these intervals by 30 seconds a week to a maximum of 5 minutes.

Right: Breaking away in a race involves riding at a hard effort over a long time.
Far right: Cycling athlete and Olympic competitor Nicole Cooke in 2005, winning the Flèche Wallone, in the Ardennes town of Huy.

Super-high intensity intervals

Intervals are similar to sprints, but you'll hold the pace for a set amount of time. Ride for 90 seconds at your maximum cruising pace, which will be not far off your maximum heart rate. Rest for 5 minutes, then repeat twice. These are extremely tough sessions, and should be treated with caution. If you are having trouble holding the pace for 90 seconds, you are not ready.

Racing Training Schedule: Endurance Events

Peaking for a race, enduro or sportive is an important part of training and achieving long-term goals. For the final two months before a race, your build-up should include more and more intensive workouts as you reach a higher state of fitness.

This training schedule is designed to get you ready for a sportive or enduro that is five hours long. Complete the basic, intermediate and advanced training schedules described earlier before tackling this schedule, which extends over eight weeks.

Train smart

You need to be careful not to overtrain – enthusiasm for hard workouts is an admirable thing, but training smart always beats training hard. When you feel fatigue building to a point where you cannot complete workouts or intervals, it is time to add in some rest periods and recovery rides before tackling harder rides.

Recovery period

In the final week before the event, you can cut down on the quantity and intensity of your training, allowing your

Above: Tough and well-designed training schedules are essential to prepare you for the arduous conditions of road or mountain bike racing.

body to recover so that it is at peak fitness for your event. It should be noted that this is an extremely time-consuming schedule and is designed for people who are able, and wish, to devote more time to their cycling. It is best to choose the most convenient time to carry out this schedule, such as when you have two months in which you have no other major commitments that could deter you from your goal.

The training schedule is worked out to train your body to maximum fitness, then the intensity reduces prior to the event to allow you to recover before achieving your goal.

Left: Hill riding and some sprints can strengthen your legs and improve your general fitness in preparation for an enduro or sportive race.

Week one
MONDAY Rest

TUESDAY LSD ride 1:30, including
   Classic intervals

WEDNESDAY LSD ride 1:30

THURSDAY LSD ride 1:30, including sprints
   and long steady climbs

FRIDAY LSD ride 1:30, including
   Classic intervals

SATURDAY Recovery ride 0:30

SUNDAY LSD ride 3:30

TOTAL HOURS: 10:00

Monday is a day off. If you are feeling good, go
for a recovery ride, otherwise, this is a good
rest to let you recover before starting the rest of
the week. Tuesday and Friday have medium
distance rides including Classic intervals.

Week two
MONDAY Rest

TUESDAY LSD ride 1:30, including
   Classic intervals

WEDNESDAY LSD ride 1:30

THURSDAY LSD ride 1:30, including sprints
   and long steady climbs

FRIDAY LSD ride 1:30, including
   Classic intervals

SATURDAY Recovery ride 0:30

SUNDAY LSD ride 4:00

TOTAL HOURS: 10:30

Similar to week one, with a day of rest on
Monday. Sunday's ride is longer. On Friday, you
may be tired from four consecutive days of
riding, so be prepared to cancel the intervals
and go for a recovery ride instead.

Week three
MONDAY Rest

TUESDAY LSD ride 1:30, including
   Classic intervals

WEDNESDAY LSD ride 2:00

THURSDAY LSD ride 1:30, including sprints
   and long steady climbs

FRIDAY LSD ride 1:30, including
   Classic intervals

SATURDAY Recovery ride 0:30

SUNDAY LSD ride 4:00

TOTAL HOURS: 11:00

Sunday's long ride stays at 4:00 to allow the
body to get used to the distance before
increasing again in two weeks. If you have
time on the Wednesday, add an extra half
hour to the ride.

Week four
MONDAY Rest

TUESDAY LSD ride 1:00, including
   spinning drills

WEDNESDAY LSD ride 1:00

THURSDAY Recovery ride 0:30

FRIDAY LSD ride 1:00

SATURDAY Recovery ride 0:30

SUNDAY LSD ride 3:00

TOTAL HOURS: 7:00

After three very hard weeks, with very
long hours of training, it is time that
you have an easy week, to allow your
body to recover its strength. Even if you
feel full of energy, do not be tempted to
train hard through this week, to avoid
the risk of overtraining.

Week five
MONDAY Rest

TUESDAY LSD ride 1:30, including
   Classic intervals

WEDNESDAY LSD ride 2:00

THURSDAY LSD ride 1:30, including short
   steep hill repetitions

FRIDAY Recovery ride 0:30

SATURDAY Long varied endurance ride 4:30

SUNDAY LSD ride 1:30

TOTAL HOURS: 11:30

The longest ride switches to Saturday, with a
long varied endurance ride of four and a half
hours, followed the next day by one and a half
hours of steady riding. This will improve
efficiency and endurance, while the intervals
and hill repetitions will boost top-end fitness.

Week six
MONDAY Rest

TUESDAY LSD ride 1:30, including
   Classic intervals

WEDNESDAY LSD ride 2:00

THURSDAY LSD ride 1:30, including
   short steep hill repetitions

FRIDAY Recovery ride 0:30

SATURDAY Long varied
   endurance ride 5:00

SUNDAY LSD ride 1:30

TOTAL HOURS: 12:00

This is the hardest week's training of all. Hill
riding will sharpen your legs and there is a
long ride on Saturday. After this week, you
will start to reduce your training volume in
order to peak for your event.

Week seven
MONDAY Rest

TUESDAY LSD ride 1:30, including
   Classic intervals

WEDNESDAY LSD ride 1:00

THURSDAY LSD ride 1:30

FRIDAY Recovery ride 0:30

SATURDAY LSD ride 1:30, including short
steep hill repetitions

SUNDAY LSD ride 2:00

TOTAL HOURS: 8:00

Reduce volume this week, with slightly shorter
long steady distance training rides on every
day except Monday, which is a day of rest,
but maintain the high intensity of Tuesday
and Friday's intervals. Include short steep hill
climbing repetitions on Saturday.

Week eight
MONDAY Rest

TUESDAY LSD ride 1:00, including
   spinning drills

WEDNESDAY LSD ride 1:00

THURSDAY Recovery ride 0:30

FRIDAY Recovery ride 0:30

SATURDAY Recovery ride 0:30

SUNDAY EVENT

TOTAL HOURS: 3:30

Another easy week with the shortest hours
put into training. The training you undertake
this week should see you ready for your event
on the Sunday. Long steady distance rides
and a recovery ride will leave you ready to
go. Just spin the legs nice and easily during
your rides this week.

*Above: Your training schedule will help
you to acquit yourself well in the event.*

Racing Training Schedule: Short-distance Events

For a shorter race, such as a local-level road race or mountain bike race, the volume of training need not be so high, but the intensity needs to be greater. When you are saving energy by doing fewer long rides, you will be able to focus on interval training.

Training for short-distance events is less time-consuming than training for longer events – the focus is on intensity rather than endurance. But it's still important to have a balanced schedule, with long rides and interval training.

Events of around 1 or 2 hours are the staple diet of most amateur racers. Both road races and mountain bike cross-country events are around this length and the shorter distance and time spent on the bike means that the racing is more intense, so your training has to reflect this. There's little point in focusing your physical and mental energy on 5-hour training rides, if events that are important to you last for less than half that time. However, endurance training is of some use. Your training base should have incorporated plenty of long rides, since the endurance you build here will make your body more able to deal with the harder, more intense training that

Above: For an event like this one, in which you will need plenty of intensive effort to climb the hill, your training will stand you in good stead.

comes in the build-up to a race. Then, during a racing period, occasional rides of up to the same time as your target races will help maintain your endurance. The main difference between training for long events like enduros or sportives, and cross-country and road races, however, is in the intensity of the training sessions. Short races can involve intense efforts, and you must make such efforts in your training so that you can replicate them in a race.

This eight-week training schedule focuses on doing two or three more

intensive sessions a week. Everything in between should be at a more steady rate, and if fatigue builds, it is far better to go for a very easy recovery ride, or even take the day off the bike, so that you will be recovered for your next intensive session. These sessions should be as varied as possible, involving sprints, intervals on flat roads, and hard efforts on hilly terrain.

If you are aiming to compete in a flat road race, focus your training on sprints and intervals on flat roads. For a hilly road race or cross-country, train on the terrain you will encounter in the race. Your interval training should build gradually, so that you increase the length of your efforts.

Left: You should train in all weathers, to be prepared for whatever conditions prevail on the day of your event.

Week one

MONDAY Rest

TUESDAY LSD ride 1:00, including Classic intervals

WEDNESDAY LSD ride 1:30

THURSDAY LSD ride 1:00, including long steady climbs

FRIDAY Recovery ride 0:30

SATURDAY LSD ride 1:30, including Classic intervals

SUNDAY LSD ride 2:30

TOTAL HOURS: 8:00

From Tuesday, the days alternate between intense training and steady training. If you are feeling good, you can add sprints and jumps or spinning drills.

Week two

MONDAY Rest

TUESDAY LSD ride 1:00, including Classic intervals

WEDNESDAY LSD ride 1:30

THURSDAY LSD ride 1:30, including long steady climbs

FRIDAY Recovery ride 0:30

SATURDAY LSD ride 1:30, including Classic intervals

SUNDAY LSD ride 2:30

TOTAL HOURS: 8:30

The schedule is basically the same as week one, with a slightly longer ride on Thursday, but you can increase the length of your intervals from week to week.

Week three

MONDAY Rest

TUESDAY LSD ride 1:00, including Classic intervals

WEDNESDAY LSD ride 1:30

THURSDAY LSD ride 1:30, including sprints and long steady climbs

FRIDAY Recovery ride 0:30

SATURDAY LSD ride 1:30, including Classic intervals

SUNDAY LSD ride 2:30

TOTAL HOURS: 8:30

The schedule is virtually the same as week two, but you can increase the length of your intervals again. Sprints have been added on Thursday.

Week four

MONDAY Rest

TUESDAY LSD ride 1:00, including spinning drills

WEDNESDAY LSD ride 1:00

THURSDAY Recovery ride 0:30

FRIDAY LSD ride 1:00

SATURDAY Recovery ride 0:30

SUNDAY LSD ride 2:30

TOTAL HOURS: 6:30

After three intensive weeks of riding, you now need to allow the body to have some recovery time.

Do not be tempted to train hard through this week or you will be vulnerable to overtraining. Instead ride steadily or at a recovery pace for the week.

Week five

MONDAY Rest

TUESDAY LSD ride 1:30, including Classic intervals

WEDNESDAY LSD ride 1:30

THURSDAY LSD ride 1:30, including short steep hill repetitions

FRIDAY Recovery ride 0:30

SATURDAY Long varied endurance ride 3:00, including sprints

SUNDAY LSD ride 1:30

TOTAL HOURS: 9:30

The week builds up through steady rides and a recovery ride on Friday. Then Saturday's ride becomes the longest of the week, incorporating high intensity sprints, followed by a steady ride on Sunday.

Week six

MONDAY Rest

TUESDAY LSD ride 1:30, including Classic intervals

WEDNESDAY LSD ride 1:30

THURSDAY LSD ride 1:30, including short steep hill repetitions

FRIDAY Recovery ride 0:30

SATURDAY Long varied endurance ride 3:00, including sprints

SUNDAY LSD ride 1:30

TOTAL HOURS: 9:30

The schedule has a similar pattern to week five, but try to raise the intensity of your intervals and climbing sessions. After this week, you can reduce training volume in order to peak for your event.

Week seven

MONDAY Rest

TUESDAY LSD ride 1:30, including Classic intervals

WEDNESDAY LSD ride 1:00

THURSDAY LSD ride 1:30

FRIDAY Recovery ride 0:30

SATURDAY LSD ride 1:30, including Classic intervals and short steep hill repetitions

SUNDAY LSD ride 2:00

TOTAL HOURS: 8:00

With two weeks to go, the week consists of a rest, steady rides with some short hill climbs. Reduce the volume of training this week, but maintain a high intensity for the intervals on Tuesday and Saturday and for climbing sessions.

Week eight

MONDAY Rest

TUESDAY LSD ride 1:00, including Classic intervals

WEDNESDAY LSD ride 1:00

THURSDAY Recovery ride 0:30

FRIDAY LSD ride 1:00, including some spinning drills

SATURDAY Recovery ride 0:30

SUNDAY EVENT

TOTAL HOURS: 4:00

An easy week in which you should wind down and get ready for your event on the Sunday. Take a rest on Monday, ride intervals on Tuesday, then spend the rest of the week spinning the legs nice and easily to taper for your event.

Above: Intensity of effort, rather than endurance, is needed for short races.

Advanced Refuelling

Cycling is an energy-intensive activity. Racing, competing and riding seriously all burn up a lot of calories, and it is often necessary to eat on the bike. It's important to consume high-energy products such as energy gels and bars, and drink enough water.

It is impractical to eat a three-course meal in the middle of a bike race. On-the-bike nutrition needs to be more accessible and easier to eat. Directly after a race, the stomach is not ready to absorb food in its raw state – it is much easier and better to rely on easy-to-digest recovery drinks. Here are some ideas of what to eat and drink on the bike to avoid an energy crash.

Water

Staying hydrated is very important, and this can be difficult, especially on hot days. When exercising in the heat you lose a great deal of water, and it is essential to replace it. Dehydration can lead to a significant dip in performance, followed by a significant dip in health, such as headaches and cramps.

By planning effectively, you can help yourself avoid dehydration. Drink plenty of water the evening before, and an adequate amount on the morning of your long ride or event. Just before the start, drink 300ml (½ pint) of fluid.

For the ride, prepare by carrying bottles, and if possible, organizing replacement bottles during a feed zone. It is better to err on the side of caution by drinking too much liquid and needing to urinate than to risk becoming dehydrated.

Energy drinks

As well as water, it is a good idea to consume energy drinks during exercise. These provide very quick energy compared with solid food, containing glucose for the muscles to use. This is important after an hour of exercise, when glycogen stores begin to drop.

Energy drinks come in powders that athletes can mix themselves with water. They consist of glucose, glucose polymers (polysaccharides), fructose, maltodextrin and any combination of

Below: During a race stay hydrated and maintain energy levels by drinking energy drinks on the go.

Above: Mix your own energy drinks from commercial powders and water. Try different brands to see which you prefer.

the above, which are easily absorbed. It is best to use the concentrations recommended by the manufacturers, although some people can tolerate different concentrations. Experiment during training with different mixes, and see what works best for you – a race or event is never the time to try something new, as your stomach may react badly.

Energy bars
Just as your body needs fluids during exercise, so it needs solid food. Food for a race needs to be portable, digestible, nutritious and high in energy. There are two ideal solutions to this – bananas and energy bars.

Above: Try different concentrations of energy drink – what works best for someone else may not suit you.

Energy bars are very popular among cyclists, and they pack quite a punch with their energy content. You should aim for a product that is easy to chew, easy to digest, and is composed of about 80 per cent carbohydrate, 10 per cent protein and 10 per cent fat. Because they are so dense and concentrated, it is essential to drink plenty of water or low concentrate energy drink with an energy bar, or you may have trouble digesting and absorbing the energy.

Below left and below: Always carry a drink attached to your bike so you can reach it while riding along.

Above: Gels provide a direct hit of energy. If your gel is not isotonic, make sure you drink water with it.

Energy gels
Because they are convenient small sachets, and contain energy-rich substances, energy gels are popular. Gels are easier to digest than an energy bar – they require no chewing and can be swallowed straight down. If the energy gel you use is isotonic, you will not need to drink water with it to ensure digestion. Some products need large quantities of fluid to be taken at the same time. Make sure you know about the product you are using and how many to take.

Below: Energy bars are ideal for long events, providing lots of fuel in a compact package.

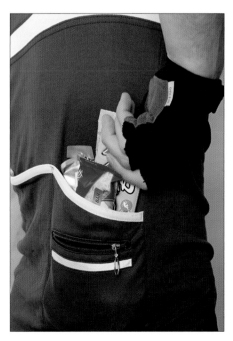

Injuries

Accidents are inevitable when you are cycling. At some point you will come off your bike or have a collision with another rider or an obstacle. There are also injuries caused by the general wear and tear that cycling inflicts on the body.

There are two major types of injuries for the typical cyclist. The first are caused by crashes. Injuries from crashes can range from a couple of scratches to, in the worst and rarest of circumstances, death. Most come somewhere in between. The second is the type of chronic injury suffered by riders through incorrect positioning or overtraining, and include bad backs and muscle strains – these tend to be less immediately painful than the first kind of injury, but they can keep you off the bike for extended periods of time.

Abrasions

For minor skin loss suffered in a crash, you can treat yourself. If you lose a lot of skin, it is a better idea to go to the hospital to get your wounds treated.

It is important, even with minor grazes and abrasions, to clean the wound thoroughly. Wounds are susceptible to infection, which can lead to illness and time off the bike. It is also important to make sure that you have had a tetanus booster in the last 10 years. If not, get one as soon as you can.

Soap and water is an adequate way of cleaning a wound, although some products are available from pharmacies to do the same job. Use a clean, sterile cloth and ensure that all the dirt is out of the wound. Once it is clean, cover it with a dressing that can be held in place with a bandage.

Broken bones

Collar bones, and to a lesser extent wrists, are susceptible to breakage in the event of a crash. When a cyclist goes down, his or her reflex is to break their fall with their hand, which can break the wrist or collarbone. If you do suffer a broken bone, you need medical attention – go to a hospital.

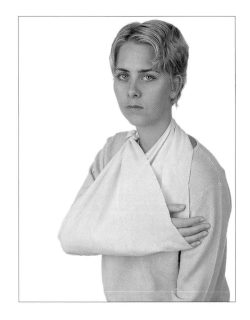

Above: Broken collarbones and arms mean extended periods off the bike. Below: Crashes are relatively common in road races – do everything you possibly can to avoid them.

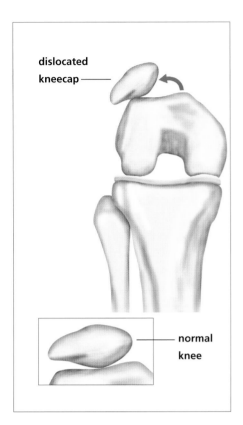

Above: The red arrow shows the direction in which the patella has dislocated. The knee joint is prone to overuse injuries – make sure your knees are aligned before pedalling.

Knee pain

All it takes is for your shoeplate to be slightly misaligned, or your saddle height to be a couple of millimetres out, or, as is more common than many people realize, your legs to be a slightly different length from each other. The repetitive nature of the cycling action will eventually exacerbate any of these problems and more, until you have chronic knee pain that prevents you from cycling.

The first thing to do when you have an injury like this is to stop cycling, which can be frustrating if you have been working hard for weeks or months. Rest, and an ice-pack on the knee, will address the immediate problem of pain and swelling. To cure the knee pain, you need to see a physiotherapist, who can assess what the root of the problem may be. Even though the pain is in your knee, the problem might be somewhere else in your body. A good physiotherapist will be able to work out why you are getting knee pain. Follow the exercise programme set for you by your physio, in order to strengthen whatever

weakness is causing the knee pain, and you should be able to resume cycling within a matter of days or weeks.

Back pain

Cyclists suffer from back pain not because cycling is inherently bad for the back, but because their position or posture on the bike is putting pressure on their lower back. If your back aches during and after long rides, try to adjust your position so you are more upright, and hold the handlebars in different positions to prevent stiffness. Also, work on your core muscles to strengthen your lower back and abdomen.

Saddle sores

Cyclists spend a lot of time sitting on a narrow saddle, which puts pressure on and causes friction in their saddle area. Minute abrasions caused by the friction can become infected, leading to a saddle sore. Prevention is much better than cure. Before every ride, treat the padded insert of your shorts with antiseptic cream, and wash scrupulously after a ride. This will prevent a painful problem farther down the line.

Above: Cyclists are liable to have backache if they have bad or incorrect posture. This can lead to a curved spine.

Above: Being aware of your posture and standing up straight can help strengthen the back and abdominal muscles.

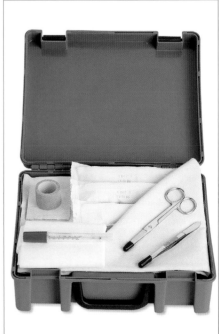

Above: Your first aid kit should contain dressings, antiseptic wipes, bandages, scissors and adhesive tape.

Resources

Further reading

SPORT

Dugard, Martin, *Chasing Lance* (Time Warner Books, London, 2005)

Fife, Graeme, *Inside the Peloton* (Mainstream, Edinburgh, 2002)

Fife, Graeme, *Tour de France: The History, the Legends, the Riders* (Mainstream, Edinburgh, 1999)

Fotheringham, William, *A Century of Cycling* (Mitchell Beazley, London, 2003)

Fotheringham, William, *Put Me Back On My Bike* (Yellow Jersey Press, London, 2002)

Fotheringham, William, *Roule Britannia* (Yellow Jersey Press, London, 2006)

Lazell, Marguerite, *Tour de France: A Hundred Years of the World's Greatest Cycle Race* (Carlton, London, 2003)

Rendell, Matt, *A Significant Other* (Weidenfeld and Nicolson, London, 2004)

Schweikher, Erich, *Cycling's Greatest Misadventures* (Casagrande, San Diego, 2007)

Watson, Graham, *Landscapes of Cycling* (Velopress, Boulder, 2004)

Wheatcroft, Geoffrey, *Le Tour* (Pocket Books, London, 2003)

Whittle, Jeremy, *Le Tour: A Century of the Tour de France* (Collins, London, 2003)

Wilcockson, John, *The World of Cycling* (Velopress, Boulder, 1998)

Woodland, Les, *The Crooked Path to Victory* (Cycle Publishing, San Francisco, 2003)

Woodland, Les, *The Yellow Jersey Companion to the Tour de France* (Yellow Jersey Press, London, 2003)

GENERAL

Andrews, Guy, *Road Bike Maintenance* (A&C Black, London, 2008)

Ballantine, Richard, *Richard's 21st Century Bicycle Book* (Pan, London, 2000)

Franklin, John, *Cyclecraft* (The Stationery Office, 1997)

Joyce, Dan, *The CTC Guide to Family Cycling* (James Pembroke Publishing, Bath, 2008)

Roberts, Tony, *Cycling: An Introduction to the Sport* (New Holland, London, 2005)

Seaton, Matt, *On Your Bike* (Black Dog Publishing, London, 2006)

Zinn, Lennard, *Zinn and the Art of Road Bike Maintenance* (Velopress, Boulder, 2000)

TRAINING

Bean, Anita, *The Complete Guide to Strength Training* (A & C Black, London, 2001)

Bompa, Tudor, *Periodization Training for Sports* (Human Kinetics, Champaign, 2005)

Burke, Edmund, *Serious Cycling* (Human Kinetics, Champaign, 2002)

Eberle, Suzanne, *Endurance Sports Nutrition* (Human Kinetics, Champaign, 2007)

Fiennes, Ranulph, *Fit For Life* (Little, Hethersett, 1999)

Friel, Joe, *The Cyclist's Training Bible* (Velopress, Boulder, 1997)

Janssen, Peter, *Lactate Threshold Training* (Human Kinetics, Champaign, 2001)

Kauss, David, *Mastering Your Inner Game* (Human Kinetics, Champaign, 2001)

Sleamaker, Rob, and Browning, Ray, *Serious Training for Endurance Athletes* (Human Kinetics, Champaign, 1996)

Wenzel, Kendra, and Wenzel, René, *Bike Racing 101* (Human Kinetics, Champaign, 2003)

Websites

www.cyclingweekly.co.uk
www.cyclingnews.com
www.bikeradar.com
www.velonews.com

Magazines

GENERAL

Cycling Plus
Bicycling

ROAD RACING

Cycling Weekly
Cycle Sport
Procycling
Velonews
Rouleur

MOUNTAIN BIKING

MBR
Mountain Biking UK

Index

CREDITS AND ACKNOWLEDGEMENTS

The publisher would like to thank the following picture libraries for the use of their pictures in the book. Every effort has been made to acknowledge the pictures properly. We apologize if there are unintentional omissions, which will be corrected in future editions.

l=left, r=right, t=top, b=bottom, c=centre

Andy Jones: 20tr, 26, 28br, 66, 67, 68 (both), 69 (both), 70t, 71c, 71br, 73tl, 76, 77 (both), 80, 81, 83 (both).
Corbis: 14, 44br, 46, 47bl, 48br, 59tr, 59br, 71t.
Geoff Waugh: 10, 50, 51, 52, 53 (all), 54 (both), 55 (all), 56 (both), 57 (all), 58 (all), 59bl, 96.
iStockphoto: 91tr.
Larry Hickmott: 66, 72t, 73br, 73t.
Offside: 6, 7, 8, 9b, 22, 38br, 42 (both), 43 (all), 44 tl, 44tr, 44bl, 45 (all), 47tl, 47t, 48t, 48bl, 49 (both), 92b.
Philip O'Connor: 9 (both), 12 (all), 13 (all), 15 (all), 16 (all), 17 (all), 20bl, 21, 23, 24 (both), 25tr, 25bl, 25br, 26bl, 27 (all), 27t, 29 (both), 30 (both), 31 (all), 32, 33 (all), 34, 35 (all), 36 (both), 37 (both), 38t, 38bl, 39 (all), 60, 61 (all), 62, 63 (all), 64 (all), 65 (all), 70bl, 70br, 72b, 73b, 74t, 75 (both), 76, 77 (both), 78 , 79 (both), 80, 82, 84, 85 (all), 86 (both), 87, 88 (both), 89, 90, 91tl, 91tc, 91bl, 91bc, 91br, 93bl, 94, 95 (both).
Superstock: 25tl, 93bc.
Triathlon magazine: 40 (both), 41 (all).